Tea Time in Alberta

Tea Time
IN ALBERTA

54 Great Tea Houses
FROM GRANDE PRAIRIE TO WATERTON LAKES

Mary Oakwell

BlueCOUCH**Books**

National Library of Canada Cataloguing in Publication Data
Oakwell, Mary, 1947-
Tea time in Alberta : 54 great tea houses from Grande Prairie to
Waterton Lakes / Mary Oakwell.

ISBN 1-894739-01-9

1. Tearooms—Alberta—Guidebooks. 2. Afternoon teas—Alberta.
3. Alberta—Guidebooks. I. Title.
TX907.5.C22A44 2003   647.957123   C2003-910236-X

Cover image: www.mikesteinhauer.com
All interior photos are by Mary Oakwell except where indicated.
Maps: Wendy Johnson, Johnson Cartographers
Blue Couch Books and the authors disclaim any liability in negligence
or otherwise for any loss, injury or damage which may occur as a result
of reliance on any information contained in this book.

Blue Couch Books
an imprint of Brindle & Glass Publishing
www.brindleandglass.com
www.bluecouchbooks.com

Brindle & Glass is committed to protecting the environment and to
the responsible use of natural resources. This book is printed on
100% post-consumer recycled and ancient forest-friendly paper. For
more information please visit www.oldgrowthfree.com.

1 2 3 4 5 06 05 04 03

PRINTED AND BOUND IN CANADA

For my father,
who never could find a teacup
big enough to hold all the tea he wanted to drink

Contents ❧

Even though location maps are provided and were accurate at the time of printing, road numbers and roads do change over time. Make sure you get the most recent highway map possible.

Introduction ☙

Tea drinking is an ancient custom in both Eastern and Western cultures. There are many different rituals associated with tea drinking, but for most of us the important thing is a moment or two of peace and quiet, or an hour with a friend when we can relax and step off our own particular treadmill for a bit.

The tea rooms in this book all have particular charms, whether it is the warmth of the proprietor, the beauty of the location, or simply the wonderful food that is offered. I'd love to have sampled more of the goodies than I did when I was collecting information for this book, but there is a limit to everyone's capacity—even mine. I shall just have to return to them all many times, as I hope you will once you are on the tea room trail.

Deciding how to define a tea room presented its own problems; many places serve and sell tea! I decided home baking was important, as was table service. If you are looking for the tea room experience, it won't include picking up your own refreshments on a tray, with probably a hot water tap to make the tea—horrors! It really boiled (pardon the pun) down to atmosphere—the kind of atmosphere that makes you want to sit, relax, and enjoy the time out. An attractive location, pretty table settings, and the smell of home baking all contribute to the atmosphere, but the biggest contribution is usually made by the owners and their staff. These are the people who have put hours, weeks, and years of planning into creating a place that warms and welcomes you as you come in the door.

The basic teas are black, green and oolong, depending on the way the tea leaves are processed. The so-called herbal teas are not really teas at all, but tisanes, blends of the roots, stems, and leaves of plants other than Camellia Sinensis, the actual tea plant, but since herbal tea is a well-recognized term, I have used it in tea descriptions. More information about types and blends of tea, tea making, and accessories such as pots can be found starting on page 121.

The terms afternoon tea and high tea are a little confusing, too, as their current usage often differs from their origin. Afternoon tea usually comprises scones and jam, and sometimes Devonshire cream, finger (dainty) sandwiches, sweet treats, and tea. High tea includes a savoury dish, chicken pot pie or a quiche perhaps, and is what most of us would have at supper time. The sweets and pastries that make up the afternoon tea are included. There are as many versions of each of these as there are tea rooms that serve them, so you'll just have to investigate.

The only prices I have included are for the "set" (afternoon, high, cream, etc.) teas, although even these are subject to change. The dishes served at each tea room are uniquely designed and prepared and comparing prices on a Caesar salad or a scone and jam is just not very useful.

I have thoroughly enjoyed meeting all the wonderful people who own and work in these tea rooms and I sincerely hope you will make the opportunity to seek them out and enjoy what they have to offer.

Note: Since some of these tea rooms are quite small and often family-run, if you're making one of them a destination, it's a good idea to telephone first. You don't want to arrive with a growling stomach to find a note pinned to the door: "Gone to ball game, see you tomorrow!"

Read this my dears, and you will see
how to make a nice cup of tea
take teapot to kettle, not t'other way round
and when you hear that whistling sound
pour a little in the pot
just make it nice and hot.
Pour that out and put in the tea,
loose or in bags, your choice, you see.
One bag for each two cups will do
with one extra bag to make a fine brew.
Steep 3-5 minutes then pour a cup.
Then sit right down and drink it up!
      — Patricia Winchester, Afternoon Teas

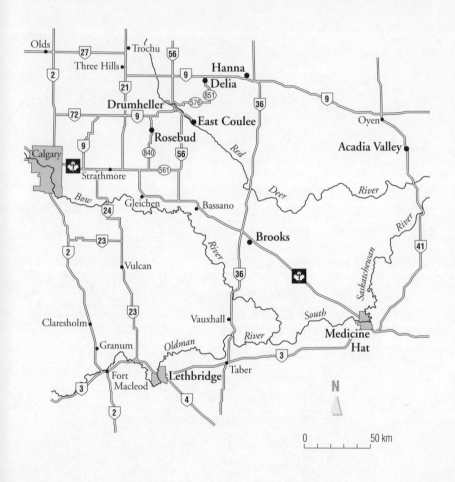

The *Palliser* Triangle

The Jasmine Room ❧

The Jasmine Room has a slightly different version of afternoon tea. Called a "Cream Tea," it includes the scone, Devonshire cream, and jam, but it also has lemon curd for that scone, as well as provolone cheese and a fresh fruit cup.

The inviting tea area is set in the midst of the gift shop and guests are encouraged to browse while they wait for their lunch or tea—someone will call them when it's ready. The casual atmosphere works with the old building that has been in the owner's family since 1917 when her grandfather operated it as a grocery business. There are three bays to the charming old building and two of them are joined by archways to house the gift shop and the tea room. The sitting area has tables and chairs for twelve and one special spot with those overstuffed armchairs that are back in fashion again.

Lunch sandwiches are served on multigrain buns or croissants with a side of fresh vegetables and dip. There is a croissant sandwich—seafood salad or ham and cheese. Other sandwiches include cucumber and egg salad and can be served with the soup of the day. The cup of soup and half sandwich combination is very popular. There is also a very good orange praline salad available. For dessert or just for a snack there is a loaf of the day, a cookie of the day, Dutch brownie squares, and butter tart squares. There is also the Bavarian fruit cup: a Bavarian chocolate cup filled with fresh fruit and topped with whipped cream.

Loose teas are served in teapots with china cups and saucers. There are black, green and herbal teas—over seventy varieties of them, including Rooibos chai and a mint flavour called Moroccan Madness. If you prefer, you can have coffee, a latte, a cappuccino or many different flavours of hot chocolate.

The store sells linens, quilts, china, pottery, flowered boxes, antiques, pictures, lamps and the wonderful items from Mary Engelbreit. Of course you can also buy the teas, the special lemon curd and, a new item to me, "t-sacs," a sort of make-your-own tea bag that just hangs in your pot and then retires to the compost heap. The Jasmine Room is a great place to slow down and enjoy a visit.

The Jasmine Room
1112 6th Avenue S, Lethbridge
T: (403) 394-9281

Hours of Operation
January–October: Tuesday–Saturday 10:00 AM–5:30 PM
November–December: Tuesday–Saturday 10:00 AM–9:00 PM

Parking: On street, free
Smoking: No
Wheelchair Accessible: Yes

Cream Tea: $5.00

Damon *Lanes* Tea Room and Gift Shop ❧

Damon Lanes Tea Room and Gift Shop is housed in a beautiful Arts-and-Crafts-style house built around 1912. The tea room is in the original living room, complete with beamed ceiling, wood floors, fireplace, and the wide wood moldings and baseboards that were so much a part of this style. The tables are set with lace cloths and flowers.

There is an incredible variety of loose teas to choose from, all clearly explained on the menu—everything from Rooibos to English Breakfast to edible fruit teas. They are all served in old-fashioned teapots, except for the Japanese teas, which appear in Japanese-style teapots.

The lunch special comprises a soup of the day (choice of two), warm whole wheat or white roll or corn muffin and then a choice of dessert—lemon cheesecake, fruit crisp or fruited white cake with hot butter sauce. Other choices are sandwiches on white, whole wheat, or rye bread (or a croissant if you prefer), pitas, or large dinner-type salads. The soups are particularly well-known—carrot orange and cabbage roll being the two favourites. The desserts, available at any time, are good-sized portions of things like German chocolate cake, cheesecake, fruit crisp, scones, carrot cake and even ice cream with strawberries.

The tea room seats twenty-five and the owners will also book showers and other special-occasion celebrations. They can do off-site catering (business lunches, for example) and have even provided box lunches for a bus tour.

The other rooms in the house are filled with gifts of all kinds. There are Crabtree & Evelyn products, Battenberg lace, pottery, a huge collection of Ty Beanies, porcelain dolls, and specialty cookbooks, to name a few. And of course the teas are available also.

Damon Lanes Tea Room and Gift Shop
730 3rd Street E, Medicine Hat
T: (403) 529-2224
www.damonlanes.com

Hours of Operation
Tea Room: Tuesday–Saturday 10:00 AM–4:00 PM
        (Lunch 11:00–2:00)
Gift Shop: Tuesday–Saturday 10:00 AM–5:00 PM

Parking: On street, free
Smoking: No
Wheelchair Accessible: Yes

The Yorkshire Rose Tea and Cake Shop 🌾

The Yorkshire Rose Tea and Cake Shop came into being when owner Sharon Tunbridge needed more space to do her wedding cakes—so the baking and cooking came naturally. All the goodies are homemade, including the marvelous chocolate eclairs. The specialty of the house is a traditional English scone served with butter, strawberry jam, and Devonshire cream.

The brunch menu includes a ploughman's lunch in the British pub style. It is made up of cheddar cheese, raw vegetables, pickled onions, fruit slice, roll and butter and, of course, Branston pickle. There are also sandwiches served on a great marble rye bread, salads, quiche, beans on toast, and toasties—sand-

wiches made waffle-style. Besides the scones and chocolate eclairs, you can choose from strawberry rhubarb pie, butter tarts or any other treat that may be a feature of the day.

Because the theme of the tea shop is Yorkshire (Sharon's husband's home) the specialty tea of the house is Yorkshire Gold—a strong black tea—but there are many more bagged teas, black and herbal, from which to choose.

Besides making and decorating wedding cakes, Sharon caters to business lunches, anniversaries and showers, or any other special occasion you can think of. An afternoon tea platter can be arranged if desired and the tea shop will remain open after hours for private parties.

The Yorkshire Rose is decorated with personal pictures of Yorkshire, from the local pub to the Abbey. Sharon sells accessories for decorating wedding cakes, but if you'd rather leave the cake making and decorating to her, you can purchase your own handmade tea cozy instead. The tea shop is right on the main street of Medicine Hat, a great place to pause for a morning or afternoon cup of tea and a few calories.

The Yorkshire Rose Tea and Cake Shop
650 3rd Street SE, Medicine Hat
T: (403) 580-3833

Hours of Operation
Monday–Saturday 9:30 AM–4:00 PM

Parking: On street, metered
Smoking: No
Wheelchair Accessible: Yes

The Prairie Elevator 🌾

It may be a bit of a trip to get to Acadia Valley but it's good to see one of these landmarks being put to such good use. The tea room building was originally the elevator office and is now an inviting place to relax. Coloured tablecloths and lace curtains are beautifully appropriate for such a building and there are prairie-type crafts and giftware displayed for you to browse through and to purchase.

The menu includes buns filled with cheese, meat and/or vegetables, all baked in the oven. There are different kinds of home-baked items such as cakes, muffins, and tarts, but the specialty of the house is pie—everything from the always-available saskatoon pie to pumpkin pie at Thanksgiving. Fruit kuchen is a favourite too. There is a wide selection of teas, but juices (saskatoon berry for one) and coffee are available if you prefer.

JUDY SCHULTZ   WWW.FOODLOVERSGUIDE.CA

The original elevator was destroyed by fire but was rebuilt in 1968, only to be considered obsolete twenty years later. A group of volunteers runs the tea room and others are there to share the history of grain production in the prairies. You can have a tour or you can wander on your own. Since the hours vary from month to month and from weekend to weekend, it would be best to call first and make sure they are open before you head out into the country.

The spirit of the tea beverage is one of peace, comfort and refinement.

— Arthur Gray

The Prairie Elevator
Main Street, Acadia Valley
T: (403) 972-2028

Hours of Operation
May 24th to Canadian Thanksgiving, call ahead

Parking: On site, free
Smoking: No
Wheelchair Accessible: Though the tea room is upstairs, the main floor is wheelchair-accessible, and tea will be brought to you there, or outside to a picnic table on the grounds

From the Prairie ❧

From the Prairie is a charming tea room, furnished with wicker chairs and mismatched tables, right in the middle of the gift shop. It's a great place to sit, relax, and look around at an incredible array of gift items. Besides being an authorized Ty Beanie dealer, Conny Scheuerman stocks many country collectibles of all kinds, a variety of pottery, the Yankee candle line, and a beautiful line of greeting cards. You can also find the Willow Tree collection of figurines, which Conny tells us is currently the number-one collectible in North America. The store is also known for its extensive collection of country-style linens.

Conny started the shop in a converted garage just outside of town. When it quickly outgrew its home, she found space in the main part of town, added the tea room, and hasn't looked back.

The menu is small but much in demand. There are different

kinds of muffins—favourites being blueberry and cranberry—as well as biscotti for the coffee drinkers. Conny often makes a specialty dessert, just to surprise the regulars. It's a great meeting spot. Teas include bagged conventional and herbal teas, all nicely served in tea pots and china mugs—chai tea is the most popular. The specialty drink isn't a tea at all, but rather a mochaccino: a shot of espresso with chocolate milk, topped with whipped cream.

It is a lovely warm place to browse for a gift, whether for yourself or someone else. When you need a break or some time to make decisions, you can sit and enjoy a cup of tea and a cranberry muffin and take all the time you need.

From the Prairie
127 1st Street W, Brooks
T: (403) 362-6650

Hours of Operation
Monday–Saturday 9:30 AM–5:30 PM

Parking: On street, also town parking lot close by, free
Smoking: No
Wheelchair Accessible: Yes

That's Crafty ❧

That's Crafty started life thirteen years ago in a little house that most people, including the building inspector, thought should be knocked down. That didn't faze owner, June Evans, who cleaned and renovated the little building, and opened with one table for four and a few shelves for locally made crafts. The tea room is now housed in the barn and has a wonderful screened-in porch from where, on a clear day, you can see the mountains.

Lunch menus vary with the season. In the summer, the salads, such as rice salad with chicken, are served surrounded by

fresh vegetables and fruit—very colourful. Croissants with turkey or ham (or a vegetarian version) are also popular. In the fall and winter, there are warmer foods and baked goods like pumpkin muffins, cranberry bread and warm gingerbread.

The pièce de résistance in the tea room is June's cinnamon bun with caramel sauce. The tea room was booked last fall to serve cinnamon buns to one hundred fire fighters on July first, but she still makes them eighteen at a time from the old recipe. Many more baked goods find their way out of the kitchen freshly made each day—rhubarb-orange coffee cake, cheesecakes, and bumbleberry crisp, as well as a "tea and cookie plate."

The crafty part of That's Crafty comprises over two thousand square feet of barn! The stalls are still there and divide the large space into cozy nooks with different themed displays from pottery and candles to stuffies and collectible kitchen ware. The tea room itself is also decorated with pictures, plaques, and ornaments for sale and, since the barn walls are so high, June decorates the upper portion with a different theme each year. The themes have been hats, weddings, children's toys and "school stuff," and always stimulate lots of interest.

That's Crafty is often part of bus tours. Once you've discovered it, you'll want to return.

That's Crafty
26 kilometres west of Drumheller on south side of Highway 9
T: (403) 677-2207
www.thatscrafty.8m.com

Hours of Operation
Monday–Saturday 10:00 AM–5:00 PM
Seasonal closings

Parking: On site
Smoking: No
Wheelchair Accessible: Yes

Murray  ea House ❧

The Murray Tea House gets its name from the Murray family who lived in it when it was a farm house in Munson. It is actually a catalogue house, ordered and built in 1919. Some structural work was needed when it was moved onto its present site a few years ago, but then it was decorated and turned into a charming tea room.

The menu, which is on the chalkboard over the counter, begins with a soup of the day and a variety of sandwiches such as crab salad and ham and cheese. These are served on rye bread or a bun. Quiche is either red pepper broccoli or spinach, and is served with a salad. For a heartier meal there is chicken pot pie or steak pot pie. Desserts include the "Decadent Brownie," cheesecakes and fudge cake, and there is also a variety of pies:

cherry, strawberry rhubarb and saskatoon. On a hot day you might prefer a sundae or a waffle cone to finish off your lunch.

Teas are Stash bagged teas served with a cup and saucer, and there are cold drinks and coffee also. The Stash teas are available for sale.

Since the tea house is on the same property as the Homestead Museum, you can enjoy a visit there too. It features early Canadiana, including small household goods, toys and fashions of earlier years.

In tea the host is simplicity and the guest elegance.
— *Matsudaira Naritada*

Murray Tea House
Highway 56, north of the river in Drumheller
T: None in the tea house; Homestead Museum is (403) 823-2600

Hours of Operation
May 15–September 30: 11:00 AM–5:00 PM daily

Parking: On site, free
Smoking: No, although there are picnic tables outside
Wheelchair Accessible: Yes

The Whistling Kettle

The Whistling Kettle is located in downtown Drumheller, opposite the unavoidable "World's Largest Dinosaur." The building dates back to at least 1914 and has been renovated and decorated to a warm and inviting atmosphere. The veranda was recently added to give additional seating in the warmer months; it doubles the Whistling Kettle's capacity to fifty people.

The menu is what the owner calls "homemade plain fare," the kind of made-from-scratch meals that mum used to make. There are always hot dishes such as quiche, taco pie, and macaroni and cheese, as well as a daily homemade soup and tea biscuit.

Salads are on the menu too. Desserts are a real specialty, number one being the sour cream rhubarb pie. Others may include lemon meringue pie and an old-fashioned pineapple cake. Karen-Lee, the owner, is always looking through recipe books for new things that will appeal to her customers.

Bagged teas are served in individual tea pots with china cups and saucers. Both black teas and herbals are available. Karen-Lee has also been researching an afternoon tea possibility that will be available with advance reservations.

The Whistling Kettle also has a country-themed gift shop with both locally made and other gift items. Some of the items you can find are baby quilts and other hand-sewn items, as well as wood crafts such as benches and birdhouses. It's a great place to go and rest from dinosaur hunting. If you order in advance, you can even take a whole pie home to share with the rest of the family.

There is no trouble so great or grave
that cannot be much diminished
by a nice cup of tea.
  — *Bernard-Paul Heroux, Basque philosopher*

The Whistling Kettle
109 Centre Street, Drumheller
T: (403) 823-9997

Hours of Operation
Monday–Saturday 8:00 AM–5:00 PM
After Labour Day: Tuesday–Saturday 8:00 AM–5:00 PM

Parking: On site, free
Smoking: No, except on veranda
Wheelchair Accessible: Yes, ramp at back door

Willow Tea Room ✿

In the '30s and '40s this great old brick school served a community of four thousand people. Those were the boom days for coal mining. By 1952 the coal mines in the valley were closing down and the school itself closed in 1972. Some forward-thinking people obtained a grant in 1986 to open the school as a museum and in 1994 the old grade five classroom became the tea room. The blackboards are still there, with chalked poems and inspirational messages. The huge windows are still there, too, for dreaming out of, but now, as well as the view, they showcase an array of pictures and memorabilia.

Now, instead of twenty or thirty grade fives, there are tables and chairs ready for breakfast, lunch or tea. Breakfast is a well-cooked bacon, eggs, hashbrowns and toast that makes the tea room a popular destination in the mornings. Lunches consist of a choice of daily soup specials, and sandwiches such as grilled cheese, roast beef, BLT, and even "hoodoo" peanut butter and jam. You can find bagels and cream cheese, salads or the ever popular "miner's lunch" that was suggested by one of the former miners from the Hungarian community. (See recipes on page 132.)

Apple pie is always on the go, as well as one other pie, depending on the season. Then there is a "fruit of the day cobbler," butter scones served with butter and jam, and ice cream or old-fashioned ice cream floats. There are twenty-one kinds of tea, both loose (Murchie's) and in bags; everything from decaffeinated to herbal to chai to black teas, all made in preheated pots and served with china cups and saucers. The iced tea is brewed on site and is unsweetened, popular with both American and European visitors. Coffee and cold drinks are available too.

When you have finished your meal or your snack, you can walk down the wide old corridors and experience some more nostalgia in the museum.

Willow Tea Room
East Coulee
T: (403) 822-3970

Hours of Operation
May 1–September 30: 9:00 AM–6:00 PM daily
March, April and October: Monday–Friday: 9:00 AM–5:00 PM

Parking: On street, free
Smoking: No
Wheelchair Accessible: Yes

Mother Mountain Tea House and Country Store ❧

This tea house is located in the old Crown Lumber building built in 1914. The early pictures of the building and of its renovation are in a scrapbook that you may want to see. There was no plumbing at all when Yvon and Heidi bought it, but, doing most of the work themselves, they opened their tea room and gift shop in 1996, two years later.

There is an extensive menu including such items as chicken pot pie, lasagna, chicken or beef wraps, and a daily chef's special. There are lighter choices as well, such as cheese toast, hot or cold sandwiches, and a Caesar salad. A favourite at Mother Mountain is one of the three individual quiches, served with salad. On

Friday nights there is a very special set meal of Texas-style baby back ribs, and on Sundays you'll find a roast beef dinner accompanied by fresh-baked bread.

The fresh homemade desserts are in the cooler for you to select your favourite—cheesecake, apple strudel and all kinds of pies, the general favourite being saskatoon berry pie. Teas include a variety of Salt Spring loose teas and some other choices of bagged teas.

The tea room can seat

thirty people, and there's also a just-completed private dining room for twelve. Heidi says it's ready for the next time the Western Premiers come to visit, although they seemed happy enough in the tea room.

In the gift area, there are gifts, crafts, collectibles, and dolls for sale. The whole building is full of charm—wood tables, chairs, and floors, wainscotting, high ceilings and lace, and shutters on the windows. It's a very charming renovation of an old commercial building.

> *Tea for two, and two for tea,*
> *Me for you, and you for me.*
>> — *Irving Caesar,* "*Tea for Two*"

Mother Mountain Tea House and Country Store
102 1st Avenue W (Main Street), Delia
T: (403) 364-2057

Hours of Operation
Mid-May to mid-October: Wednesday–Sunday 11:00 AM–8:00 PM
Valentine's Day to mid-May: weekends only

Parking: On street, free
Smoking: No, except outside on patio
Wheelchair Accessible: Yes

The Doll Palace Tea Room ❧

The Doll Palace Tea Room is housed in a fairly new building with a real prairie feeling. It's right on the edge of town but nobody has any trouble finding it. Many local people pick up Violetta's phenomenal cinnamon buns on the way to work. The tea room is open officially at 8:00 AM, but the crew is there early, and if the cinnamon buns are ready earlier they are out the door.

It's a family business; a very busy one. The menu is up on the white board: a special of the day plus a choice of two homemade soups and open-faced sandwiches on homemade buns. The locals know that Friday is chicken day—browned first, then finished in

the oven and served with potatoes, vegetables and gravy. On Sundays the buffet usually includes roast beef served from 11:00 AM to 2:00 PM, and from 4:30 to 6:00 PM. In the summer the produce is from the garden behind the tea room.

From the buffet Violetta often makes up dinners to go, especially for the seniors who can't get out. There's an incredible range of pies either to go or to eat there: rhubarb, cherry, raisin, blueberry, chocolate, and flapper pie—which, for the uninitiated, is a graham wafer crust and vanilla filling topped with meringue. Then there are the cakes: butter pecan and angel cake with strawberries are the favorites. The tea room also takes another step into the past by serving floats: a scoop of ice cream in your favorite pop, absolutely perfect for a hot day. There is a variety of bagged teas available, always served in a pot with cups and saucers.

The doll palace is actually a museum of over four thousand dolls. There is a small admission charge to the museum, but it is well worth it. The oldest doll is from the 1890s and there are over seventy-five doll companies represented—everything from babies to Barbies.

The gift shop is not large but quilts made from old jeans could tempt you. And you'll be pleased to find a listing of upcoming local events on each table, if you plan to stay awhile.

The Doll Palace Tea Room
400 Pioneer Trail, Hanna
T: (403) 854-2756

Hours of Operation
Wednesday–Sunday 8:00 AM–6:00 PM

Parking: On site, free
Smoking: Yes
Wheelchair Accessible: Yes

That Country Place ❦

An old 1920s house that had outlived itself as a home was sitting up on skids near Stettler when Dawna and Darrell Motz first saw it and thought it would make a perfect tea room and bed and breakfast. They bought it, moved it to their farm, and attached it to the shop area they had already built. It is now beautifully renovated with stained glass windows, the old wood floors and doors, and traditional floral wallpaper.

Daily specials include items like chicken in puff pastry, salmon bake, or chicken bake, as well as homemade soups, crois-

sants, and sandwiches. Desserts are to die for— cheesecakes, mocha revel cake, strawberry shortcake, and a cookies and cream brownie that will make your mouth water just to look at it. You always get dessert; Dawna has a little cup-and-saucer chocolate mold that makes a dear dessert which she serves after every meal.

There are approximately twenty loose teas to choose from, served in tea pots with cups and saucers. For hot days there are cold drinks—iced tea and lemonade. If you prefer coffee, it is available too.

In the gift shop you can find country and Victorian-style gifts: Lang calendars and stationery, folk art, candles, quilts and collector bears, dolls and bunnies. Teas and tea-making accessories are also available.

There are a number of special events you might want to

watch for—there's a Mother's Day contest in May and a Teddy Bear Picnic in September. Perhaps the most special is the Christmas in the Country celebration in November when the open house welcomes you with a country tree and a Victorian tree, a great variety of Christmas items for sale, and plenty of Christmas treats to eat and drink—reservations are recommended if you are staying for lunch.

While you are visiting, ask for a peek at the beautifully restored attic that is now a bed and breakfast suite. You'll want to reserve a getaway weekend for sure.

> *[Tea's] goodness is a decision for the mouth to make.*
> — *Lu Yu*

That Country Place
Five miles northeast of Hanna, on Highway 36 north
T: (403) 854-2572
www.bbexpo.com/thatcountryplace

Hours of Operation
May–December: Tuesday–Saturday 10:00 AM–5:00 PM
January–April: Wednesday–Saturday 10:00 AM–5:00 PM

Parking: On site, free
Smoking: No
Wheelchair Accessibility: Yes, there is a ramp that can be put down as necessary

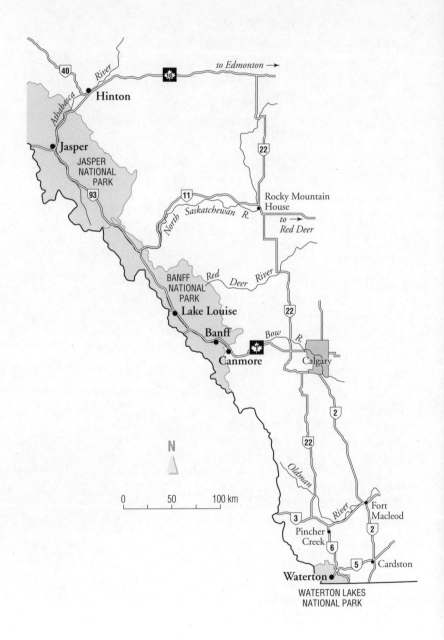

The *Rocky* Mountains

Prince of  ales Hotel

Sitting high on a bluff and surrounded by mountain peaks, the Prince of Wales Hotel was built in 1927, overlooking the township and the lake of Waterton. The food is excellent and the setting is unbelievable. The magnificent hotel is built in a Swiss style with heavy hand-hewn posts and beams. The lobby where afternoon tea is served is five stories high and features a mammoth stone fireplace.

Afternoon tea consists of scones, berries, and Devonshire cream, as well as spectacular homemade pastries.

Shops in the hotel and nearby offer lovely gift items such as English bone china, Waterford crystal and aboriginal crafts. If you feel like physical activity, it's a beautiful place for boating, hiking or horseback riding.

Prince of Wales Hotel
774 Railroad Street, Waterton Park
T: (406) 892-2525
F: (406) 892-1375
www.princeofwaleswaterton.com

Hours of Operation
June–September: 2:00 PM–4:00 PM daily

Parking: Hotel parking lot, free
Wheelchair Accessible: Yes

Afternoon Tea: Adults $30.44, Children $7.44

Fairmont *Banff* Springs Hotel ❧

The most magnificent of the early railway hotels, the Fairmont Banff Springs nestles into the mountains with incredible views on all sides. The elegant afternoon tea is served in the Rundle Lounge, overlooking the Bow Valley.

The meal begins with a fresh fruit cup and is followed by finger sandwiches such as smoked salmon and cream cheese or English cucumber. Victorian scones are served with Devonshire cream and strawberry jam, and you must definitely save room for

the fresh pastries and sweets. All this is complemented by the "Banff Springs Special Blend" tea, designed to take advantage of the deliciously fresh mountain water. It is a really delightful and relaxing treat.

Fairmont Banff Springs Hotel
405 Spray Avenue, Banff
T: (403) 762-2211

Hours of Operation
2:00 PM—4:00 PM daily

Parking: Hotel parking lot
Smoking: No
Wheelchair Accessible: Yes

Afternoon Tea: $24.95; or served with a glass of sparkling wine and including a gift tea box $34.95

Lake *Agnes* Tea House ☙

By the time you have reached this lovely rustic log cabin, you deserve whatever your heart desires. It's a 3.4 kilometre (2.1 miles) walk, all uphill from Lake Louise, and the change in elevation (as the brochure blithely reports) is 385 metres (1263

feet). This is not for the faint-hearted or the weak-kneed, but it is definitely worth the trip. Alternately, you could hire a horse to take you up a slightly different trail.

Lake Agnes is that brilliant green colour so typical of mountain lakes and is totally surrounded by mountain peaks— there really is only just room for the tea house. The lake overflows into a pretty waterfall.

Since all the supplies are trekked in by packhorse every two weeks, except for the annual helicopter delivery of staples, it is not surprising that the menu is quite small. There are sandwiches all served on freshly baked bread, soups, tea biscuits, fruit loaves and cold drinks. There are still 36 flavours of loose tea and you can have a pot for two or a pot for six. There is no coffee, but there is hot chocolate and a very delicious cold peach drink. You can also buy bottled water, especially important if you are travelling further along the trails. The chef bakes seven loaves of bread per day for the sandwiches, seven loaves of fruit bread each day, and, on the day I visited, she was just taking trays of huge cookies out of the oven.

The original log cabin was built in 1910 as a rest stop for mountain-climbing visitors. Time had taken its toll, however, and the present tea house was built in 1984. The tea room is open from June 1 until Thanksgiving weekend (Canadian, that is), and the staff stay either in the loft of the tea house or in one of the two cabins a little further up the mountainside. At the end of the season, they close up the building and trek the leftovers and the garbage back down the hill.

They serve from two to three hundred hardy souls every day, so get out your comfortable walking shoes or your hiking boots—it's an incredible spot.

Lake Agnes Tea House
3.4 kilometres up from Lake Louise
Trail begins by the lake, near the Chateau
T: Check information with the Visitor Centre
in Banff (403) 762-1550

Hours of Operation
June 1–Thanksgiving weekend in October

Parking: Horses only
Smoking: No, though you may smoke at the tables outside
Wheelchair Accessible: Definitely not

Plain of Six Glaciers Tea House ❦

The absolutely stunning view from this tea house (and on the way to it) is the best reason in the world to make the trip. You'll need all your stamina and a good pair of shoes for this one as it's at 2075m (6800 feet) above sea level, so a somewhat rarified atmosphere. Like the hike to the Lake Agnes Tea Room, you start at Chateau Lake Louise, but on this hike you gain 365 metres (1198 feet) in elevation over 5.3 kilometres (3.3 miles) —coming down is a breeze.

The menu is small but everything tastes particularly good after the long climb. The sandwiches are made with freshly baked

bread and the scones are baked daily too. There's a hearty home-made soup and some lovely desserts—chocolate cake or apple pie fresh out of the oven. Drinks include peachade, lemonade, bot-tled water, hot chocolate, coffee and, of course, tea. It's bagged tea, either orange pekoe or peppermint.

All the supplies come at the beginning of the season by hel-icopter, or by pack horse or backpack. This means that garbage and recycling has to be trekked down too. The staff live in cabins close to the tea house and most of them stay up for the whole five-month season. The stove is fuelled by propane (which the pack horses bring) and the tea room and cabins are heated by wood stoves, requiring taking turns at chopping wood.

The tea house is in the original building, built with local stone and wood, started in 1924 and completed in 1927. The business has been in the same family for forty-two years, handed down from mother to daughter. It was opened originally to provide refreshment for scrambles and mountain climbs. The kitchen is on the main floor, and food (and messages) are shipped up to the second floor by dumbwaiter.

After you've been refreshed at the tea house, you can climb another half mile and see an old hut from the very early mountain climbing days. The tea house has a very friendly atmosphere—even if you arrive after hours, someone will be around to make you a cup of tea or find you something to eat. It is a great experience, well worth the climb.

Plain of Six Glaciers Tea House
5.3 kilometres up from Lake Louise
T: Check information with the Visitor Centre
in Banff (403) 762-1550

Hours of Operation
Weather permitting: June 1–Thanksgiving weekend
in October 9:00 AM–6:00 PM

Parking: Horses only
Smoking: No
Wheelchair Accessible: Not a chance

$\mathcal{N}$orth West Mounted Police Barracks Tea Room ☞

The building in which this tea room is located is 109 years old. As its name implies, it was built as a barracks for the North West Mounted Police, the peace keepers at the turn of the century. It housed not only the police officers but also the jail and the only available courthouse until 1929. The town of Canmore purchased the building in 1989 to preserve the only remaining building of its kind on its original site. Presently there are two rooms restored (in the lean-to added at a later date) as a living room and bedroom, with a close-up view of the original logs and chinking through an interior window.

Visitors to the tea house and museum are served a pot of tea in an old-style brown pot, or a glass of iced tea or lemonade, and

a plate of cookies donated by a local bakery. The red and white checquered tablecloths, the lace at the windows, and the old stove add to the stepped-back-in-time feeling of the tea house.

The place is run by volunteers and you pay for your tea and goodies with a donation. There are maps and souvenirs for sale as well as books about the area's history, about the Rocky Mountains and about the wild animals that inhabit the terrain.

> *Peter was not very well during the evening.*
> *His mother put him to bed,*
> *and made some chamomile tea; and she gave a dose of it to Peter!*
> *'One table-spoonful to be taken at bed-time.'*
>
> *— Beatrix Potter*

North West Mounted Police Barracks Tea Room
609 Main Street, Canmore
T: (403) 678-5458 / (403) 678-5552

Hours of Operation
Summer: Wednesday–Sunday 10:00 AM–5:00 PM
Winter: Saturday and Sunday 12:00 noon–4:00 PM

Parking: On street, free
Smoking: No
Wheelchair Accessible: Yes

McCracken Country Inn ❧

Whether you're interested in breakfast, lunch, a wedding reception, a getaway weekend, or celebrating Ukrainian Christmas, Fay and Kyle McCracken will be happy to help. They also do Christmas parties, a Robbie Burns night, or organized retreats, but if you just want tea and dessert at the tea house, that's fine too.

Breakfast has all kinds of possibilities and is served from 7:00 to 11:00 each morning. Veggie scrambled eggs, Cabin Hash, omelettes and breakfast burritos as well as the old standby of eggs and bacon, toast and hashbrowns are all available. For a smaller appetite there are some bagel choices, cinnamon toast, and muffins and jam, to name just a few.

At lunch there is a homemade soup of the day served with a freshly baked scone, a variety of salads, including a Caesar and an Italian chicken salad, or sandwiches on bagels or on white, brown, or rye bread. Hot sandwiches work well for cooler days, especially the Montana Grill: turkey, bacon, tomatoes, cheese, and an avocado dressing. Quiche, quesadillas and pitas are all there too and, if you're lucky, the special of the day might just be buffalo burgers, served with all the trimmings.

For dessert there are all kinds of fruit pies, depending on the season, as well as the popular lemon meringue. The most popular of the loose teas offered is Monk's Blend, but there are many more to choose from, including Green Tea Spice Chai and Sunshine Lemon Rooibos. Tea is served in teapots kept warm by a tea cozy, with a china cup and saucer. Coffee and cold drinks are also served.

The gift shop is in the lounge of the inn and features teddy bears, gift boxes, books, teas, coffees and hot chocolates, and all the tea accessories, like cozies and strainers.

Fay also offers an afternoon tea buffet, which includes the scones and jam, fruit platter and dips, finger sandwiches and assorted dainties. You need a reservation for this one. And, if you're hoping for a tall, dark handsome stranger in your future, you may want to make an appointment for a psychic reading with Yvonne; just call Fay to make the appointment.

The rooms in the inn are charmingly decorated with gas fireplaces in each room and besides the eight rooms upstairs, there is one on the main floor which is wheelchair accessible.

McCracken Country Inn
146 Brookhart Street (a service road off Highway 16 and easily seen from the highway), Hinton
T: 1-888-865-5662 / (403) 865-5662
www.mccrackencountryinn.com

Hours of Operation
7:00 AM—4:00 PM daily

Parking: On site, free
Smoking: No
Wheelchair Accessible: Yes

Afternoon Tea buffet: $11.99, must be booked in advance

Maligne Canyon Teahouse ❧

The Maligne Canyon Teahouse is located at the top of a beautiful walk through the canyon. The walk meanders beside the river, which constantly changes level as it weaves in and out of the caves and tunnels. One of the bridges is 165 feet above the water which culminates in a magnificent waterfall.

The tea house offers both service and self-service areas in the beautiful rustic building, its huge fireplace in the middle. You can have a complete meal featuring both North American food and the Middle Eastern cuisine that is the specialty of the Lebanese chef. If you can resist the full-course menu, there is still a choice

of black or herbal teas with home-baking for snacking. Coffee is also available.

The gift and fine art gallery surrounds the eating areas and features wonderful Native Canadian and Inuit art. There are stone and ivory carvings and artwork made from tusks of the walrus and the narwhal. Bronze sculptures made in the United States are also on display. The gift shop includes jewellery, unique clothing, leather goods and books. Maligne Canyon Teahouse makes a lovely destination after a breathtaking walk along the river.

Better to be deprived of food for three days, than tea for one.
— Chinese Proverb

Maligne Canyon Teahouse
11 kilometres east of Jasper townsite, along
Highway 16, on Maligne Road
T: (780) 852-5565
www.malignecanyon.com

Hours of Operation
May: 8:00 AM–6:00 PM daily
June 1–September 1: 8:00 AM–10:00 PM daily
September 1–mid-October: 8:00 AM–6:00 PM daily

Parking: On site, free
Smoking: Outside only
Wheelchair Accessible: Yes

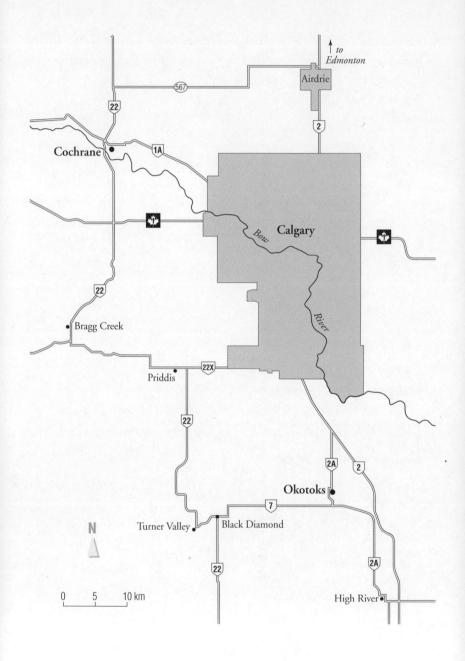

Calgary and Area

Steps the *Urban* Tea House ❧

Wonderful wall colours will catch your eye as you walk through the double doors: green, yellow, purple, and blue in lovely intense colours, a great background for a huge display of loose teas. It's a very striking décor, set off beautifully by the checkerboard wood floors.

The menu at Steeps is select, and lunch is based mostly on soup and sandwich combinations. The soups are made fresh daily and are always in demand. Sandwiches are made on either a Steeps panini or on a seven-grain bread from a new, local commercial bakery. Customers keep asking for the bread by the loaf, but at the moment you just have to enjoy it at Steeps. A large

number of salads from Tubs in Calgary are available, including the vegetarian varieties as well as a "pesto pasta" for a heartier appetite. There is usually a stew available too.

Desserts are rich and satisfying. They include things like chocolate fudge fantasy, triple layer cheesecake, and a spectacularly good carrot cake, as well as some smaller French pastry items like apricot or lemon tarts.

Over a hundred

varieties of tea are displayed for you to choose from. You can take the lids off and decide by look and by smell, and of course you can come back many times to sample others. The tea is made and served in French Presses. The teas and tea-making accessories are available for sale, so you can take a few choices home as well. There is also a line of bath and beauty products made from a tea base, as well as gifts with a tea theme. Brendan and Paul Waye, the brothers who own both the Calgary and the Edmonton Steeps, sell their chai concentrate across Canada and you can certainly pick up a supply here. If you want to know what new teas have arrived, you can find out on the Steeps website.

Note: Steeps also has an Edmonton location (see page 100).

Steeps the Urban Tea House
880 16th Avenue SW (Mount Royal)
T: (403) 209-0076
www.steepstea.com

Hours of Operation
Monday–Wednesday: 9:00 AM–11:00 PM
Thursday and Friday: 9:00 AM–12:00 midnight
Saturday: 10:00 AM–12:00 midnight
Sunday: 10:00 AM–11:00 PM

Parking: On street, metered or parkade
Smoking: No
Wheelchair accessible: Yes

Tea and *Time* Emporium ❦

Tea and Time Emporium is exactly that—a tea room and a time shop. Clocks of all kinds decorate the walls and you can even bring your own in for repairs. The clocks range from cuckoo clocks to grandfathers, and they cuckoo, strike, or play musical tunes depending on their particular insides. Their times are set differently so they don't all create at once. The tea room is decorated with blue cloths and napkins and pretty china set on old wooden chairs and tables. There is a large variety of loose teas, with a particular one featured each day.

The menu includes such things as eggs benedict and vegetable omelettes, sandwiches, wraps and melts, and different

kinds of salads. There are also many varieties of scones served with preserves and whipped cream, although Devonshire Cream is available if you prefer. For dessert there are homemade sweet loaves, pies, cream puffs, and a special light dessert called "Angel Berries." The loose teas are on display in glass jars so that you can choose by appearance and aroma, and the tea room is fully licensed.

Tea and Time serves afternoon tea, featuring sandwiches, scones and sweets. There is also a children's tea tray with little sandwiches and things more suited to younger taste buds. Another special feature of Tea and Time is palm, tea leaf, and tarot readings. A reservation for these is a good idea, although you can be lucky on a drop-in basis too.

Besides the clocks you can purchase teapots, strainers, and handmade tea cozies. The shopping centre in which the tea room is located also features a number of interesting and unique retail outlets.

> *Tea is such a magical product—perhaps even the eighth wonder of the world ...*
> — *Mr. H. Rahman, Senior Tea Buyer at Harrods*

Tea and Time Emporium
Glenmore Landing, 1600 90th Ave SW
T: (403) 258-3300

Hours of Operation
Monday–Friday: 10:00 AM–6:00 PM
Saturday: 10:00 AM–5:00 PM
Sunday: 11:00 AM–5:00 PM
Major holidays: call first

Parking: on site, free
Smoking: No
Wheelchair Accessible: Yes

Afternoon Tea: $26.00 for two people

Conversations Tea Room

The chef at Conversations Tea Room is very proud to say that he did all the cooking for Luciano Pavarotti when the latter was performing at the Calgary Saddledome. Needless to say, the food is extra-special here. The extensive lunch menu includes breakfast

all day, quiche, and Thai salad, as well as a grape and chicken salad. There is a crab melt croissant, a vegetarian sandwich with Swiss or cheddar cheese, and lox on a bagel. There are beautiful, freshly made desserts, including cheesecakes, and in the scone department there are substantial currant scones and white chocolate raspberry scones, a specialty of the house.

There are over thirty kinds of tea, including some decaffeinated ones and some with great names like Lovers' Leap. Conversations also serves herbal teas and the South African Rooibos varieties. There are even Tutti Frutti and Bubblegum flavours for children.

Conversations also serves high tea. It includes mini quiche, pastry cases filled with chicken and grape salad, sandwiches, and cheeses. On the dessert part of the tray you will find blueberry mini-scones, biscotti, fresh fruit, lemon tarts and more.

The tea room is very prettily decorated with flowered wallpaper on a blue background, lots of lace, old-fashioned lamps, and angels on the walls, another specialty of the owner. Even the washrooms are charming, with hand-painted murals and quotations on the walls.

Conversations is fully licensed and also does catering, private functions, and tea readings. The owner, Krystyna Stefan, has also hosted other functions at the tea house from fashion shows to brownie outings, and is planning to add a poetry evening (Thursdays) and a mystery dinner evening too.

The Willow Park Mall is an interesting little mall with one-of-a-kind boutiques rather than chain stores. The small gift shop in Conversations has exquisite imported linens, china and dolls, and Ms. Stefan is always on the lookout for local artisans' work. The many wall decorations throughout the tea room (including the angels) are also for sale.

Conversations Tea Room
Willow Park Shopping Centre, 10816 Macleod Trail South
T: (403) 271-8886

Hours of Operation
Monday–Wednesday, Friday–Saturday 10:00 AM–6:00 PM
Thursday 10:00 AM–8:00 PM
Sunday 10:30 AM–3:30 PM

Parking: In the mall parking lot, free
Smoking: No
Wheelchair accessible: Yes

High Tea: $24.99 for two people

Tara's Treasures

Tara's Treasures is located in a mall, but the garden ambience is felt as soon as you walk in the door. The beautiful floral drapes set off the trellised walls, and your meal is served at wrought-iron tables and chairs.

There is an interesting and extensive menu. For the morning tea or coffee break—or light refreshment any time—you can find scones, johnnycake and mini-loaves. If breakfast is on your mind, there's "Eggs Jenny ('cos we don't know Benny)," which comprises a cheddar scone, tomato, ham, poached egg, and cheese sauce. Tara's Egg Nests also are something a little differ-

ent: large eggs in a bread shell basket, oven-baked and topped with fried mushrooms, served with salsa sauce.

Lunches, too, have a twist. The spirilla salad is made with pasta and ten different vegetables marinated in balsamic vinegar. You can choose soup and a scone for a light lunch or you can have a pizza bagel, chicken strips or their ever-popular quiche. A specialty of the house is the crêpe dish: ham, chicken, shrimp, or veggies, wrapped in herbed crêpes and covered with a wine and cheese sauce. Pita pockets are available too. The dessert tray is filled with deliciously tempting cakes and cheesecakes.

Tara's Treasures serves afternoon tea between 2:00 and 4:00 PM. The tray includes sandwiches, sweets, fresh fruit cup, and scones with strawberry preserves and mock Devonshire cream. Reservations for afternoon tea are recommended.

The shop is large and filled with a great variety of china, teapots, stuffies, cards, candles, picture frames and some interesting ladies' dresses and outfits. And if your future is on your mind, you can make an appointment to have your tea leaves read.

You have arrived at a propitious moment, coincident with your country's one indisputable contribution to Western civilisation— afternoon tea.

— Hugo Drax, villian of Moonraker, to James Bond

Tara's Treasures
2404 Centre Street N
T: (403) 230-3166

Hours of Operation
Monday–Friday 10:00 AM–5:30 PM
Saturday 10:00 AM–5:00 PM
July and August: closed Mondays

Parking: On site, free
Smoking: No
Wheelchair accessible: Yes

Afternoon tea: $12.50 per person

The Saskatoon Farm

The Saskatoon Farm looks and feels like a little prairie town—a booming one, that is. In 1987 it was a barley field. Now it is covered with trees, bushes, and orchards, and comprises a U-pick operation, a farming and processing facility, a buffalo herd, a mail-order operation, and a fabulous tea room. The old-fashioned buildings sport Sheriff's Office and Saskatoon Saloon signs, and inside are the store and the tea room. Outbuildings house the garden centre, open from April 15 through October 31.

The menu is really interesting, with emphasis on buffalo and saskatoon berry items. There are buffalo burgers, smokies and burritos, all served with Caesar salad or the salad of the day,

but there is also a soup of the day served with gouda cheese and a herb biscuit, or a soup and sandwich special. If you're still in breakfast mode when you visit, you might like to try the breakfast burrito.

Desserts abound, many of them with a saskatoon berry component—saskatoon pie, of course, but cheesecake too. Then there are things like white chocolate and saskatoon scones or saskatoon ripple ice cream. Teas are Red Rose or herbals. Coffee and cold drinks are available too: the saskatoon lemonade is wonderfully refreshing on a hot day.

The garden centre carries a large selection of saskatoon bushes, shelterbelt, landscaping and fruit trees, as well as non-woody perennials, annuals and hanging baskets. The gift store has a great variety of garden ornaments, plaques, pots, and other interesting and useful things, such as wasp traps.

The farm is located three kilometres off Highway 2, and there is good signage from both directions. It is well worth a lengthy visit to browse through the garden centre and store while you work up an appetite for lunch or teatime.

The Saskatoon Farm
South of Okotoks and north of Aldersyde, east of Highway 2
T: (403) 938-6245
www.saskatoonfarm.com

Hours of Operation
9:00 AM–6:00 PM daily

Parking; On site, free
Smoking: No
Wheelchair Accessible: Yes

The Home Quarter

The Home Quarter is another one of the few tea rooms that serves an elegant afternoon tea. The smaller version includes an individual quiche, tea sandwiches, and sweets—butter tarts, shortbread and others. The larger version also includes a scone with homemade berry preserves and whipped vanilla Devonshire cream as well as an English trifle or crème caramel for dessert.

The Home Quarter also has a full breakfast and lunch menu. Breakfast ranges from bagels and coffee to a Neptune Benedict and there are special Home Quarter hotcakes on the weekends. Lunch involves a choice of two soups daily (clam chowder on

Fridays), a daily quiche and a daily special—roast beef and Yorkshire pudding the day I visited. Lots of sandwich choices can accompany your soup, ranging from a "loaded grilled cheese" to a Reuben. Croissants can be filled with a seafood medley or a pineapple coconut chicken curry. There are also different flavours of chicken burgers—for example, Carolina honey chicken—as well as Home Quarter pot roast, baked Pacific salmon, saskatoon berry chicken, and the Chef's Own meatloaf. Salads include spinach tostada, sesame chicken, or Caesar with shrimp, chicken or Alberta beef. The "cup and a half"—a cup of soup and half a sandwich—is popular for the smaller appetite.

For the sweeter tooth, there is a huge array of cheesecakes, from rum and eggnog to Jo Jo's Obsession (intrigued?), but pies are the big attraction at The Home Quarter. All forty-five varieties are sold by the piece or by the pie. Some of the choices are Texas buttermilk, cherry-raspberry, saskatoon-strawberry, and fruit medley. You can also purchase sugar-free pies, but these and the cream pies require a day's notice. If you're not in the mood for pie, you can choose an apple cinnamon wagon wheel, a butter tart, a date square, or the feature muffin of the day.

Loose teas are served in ceramic tea pots and china cups and saucers. They include Irish Cream, Arctic Raspberry and Peach Apricot, herbals like Bella Coola and Angel Falls Mist, and many others. For afternoon tea, Home Quarter uses their English Rose china and serves in the special tea room (also available at lunch time). It is a charming room with wood floors, a fireplace, and elegant molding. It is decorated with roses and lace that really complement the china.

The Home Quarter
216 1st Street (Main), Cochrane
T: (403) 932-1743
www.homequarter.nu

Hours of Operation
Weekdays: 10:00 AM–10:00 PM
Weekends and holidays 9:00 AM–10:00 PM

Parking: On street, free
Smoking: No
Wheelchair Accessible: Yes

Afternoon tea: Monday–Saturday 2:00 PM–4:30 PM, by reservation: Small $10.95, Large $16.95

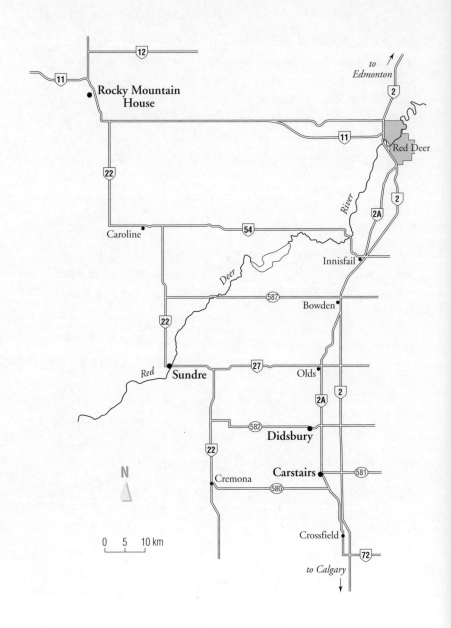

The *Foothills*

PaSu Farm

This is a lovely location on the edge of the foothills where you can have your meal or tea overlooking the rolling countryside and the grazing sheep. It is a large facility, its wood walls covered with beautiful South American tapestries and carvings.

Full lunch is served from 12:00 noon–2:00 PM and includes choices of wild mushroom soup or another daily soup, and salads fresh from the garden in season. Then there is a Mediterranean country sandwich—a quarter of a baguette filled with cheese, salami, tomatoes, and fresh herbs, as well as other sandwiches, including toasted cheese for the kids. Heartier

appetites can find grilled steak sandwich and salad, grilled lamb chops, or a PaSu pie.

Desserts are abundant—fresh-baked fruit pies and PaSu Farm scones baked fresh for each order. Profiteroles are "choux pastries filled with rich cream and served on a puddle of raspberry or strawberry purée and smothered in chocolate sauce"; Devil's Torte is as wicked as it sounds, with orange liqueur and chocolate sauce being only two of the ingredients. And, if you still haven't found what you fancy, how about a chocolate paté or a crème caramel?

The Saturday evening meal is a many-course dinner with such things as passionfruit and champagne sorbet, and chicken livers and cognac paté. The entree is a choice (which you make at reservation time) between rack of lamb and Atlantic salmon, and is served with "baby red potatoes, fresh baby carrots and snow peas."

A large number of loose teas is available: regular, fruit, herbal, and Rooibos. They are served in a preheated pot with a cup and saucer. The signature tea is called PaSu Blend and resembles an orange pekoe. Coffee and cold drinks are also available, and the tea room is fully licensed.

The gift shop has a lovely display of wool blankets and wool clothing, quilts, copperware, tapestries, metal work and some great hats. Teas are available for sale too.

PaSu Farm also caters to weddings, does special Christmas dinners and offers Friday night "pub nights."

PaSu Farm
Twenty kilometres southwest of Carstairs
T: (403) 337-2800
www.pasu.com

Hours of Operation
Tuesday–Saturday: Shop opens at 10:00 AM
Lunch 12:00 noon–2:00 PM, light lunch and desserts 2:00–4:00 PM
Friday pub nights: From 5:30 PM
Saturday: Dinner as arranged
Sunday: Lunch at 12:00 noon, final seating at 1:00 PM
Tea: 2:30 PM–4:00 PM

Smoking: No
Wheelchair Accessible: Yes

The *Tea* Cozy and Gift Shop ❧

This charming little tea room is in the middle of a residential district of Didsbury. It was for several generations a family home, protected for many years by a large hedge that was eventually discovered by the owner and the RCMP to be marijuana. It was removed forthwith. The house is still there with seating both inside and on the screened veranda for tea room customers.

The lunch menu usually includes a quiche, perhaps asparagus and feta cheese, a meat dish such as cranberry chicken, spinach and sausage pie, or leek and chicken pie, old-fashioned meatloaf, or shepherd's pie. In the summer, lunch dishes are accompanied by a salad, in spring and fall by hot vegetables, and always by a homemade tea biscuit. Soups are also available in cooler weather.

The desserts are wonderful to complete lunch or to have in the afternoon with a cup of tea. They vary from day to day but could include pumpkin pie, pecan pie, crème caramel, raspberry or blueberry cheesecake, or Tea Cozy's special version of rice pudding. Another special Tea Cozy creation is chocolate cake with homemade chocolate syrup, whipped cream and ice cream.

The many teas are loose and are served in hand-painted teapots and cups and saucers.

Coffee (made from bottled water) and cold drinks are also available. Reservations are a good idea and they give you an opportunity to request your favourite foods, particularly those desserts.

The gift shop displays in the front entrance and the hallways offer lots of choices. There are candles, topiary and flower arrangements, stained glass, pictures, pillows, lamps, stuffies and, of course, tea cozies. Salt Spring teas are also for sale.

Tea and books—Mmmmmm, two of life's exquisite pleasures that together bring near-bliss.

— Christine Hanrahan

The Tea Cozy and Gift Shop
1510 21st Avenue, Didsbury
T: (403) 335-8090

Hours of Operation
April–December Tuesday–Saturday 11:00 AM–5:00 PM
Closed January and February; in March tea room is closed but gift shop and stained glass studio are open—tea and coffee are available

Smoking: No
Wheelchair Accessible: No

22-*Birdwalk* Tea and Crafts

If you enjoy quiet trails and the possibility of finding thirty-two species of birds at the bird feeders, you will particularly enjoy the 22-Birdwalk tea room. Hilda Gamble and Norm Loppe have seen every species from hummingbirds to great grey owls, and they want to keep attracting all of them. The rustic tea room looks over a pretty garden, tables are dressed in plaid tablecloths and there's an old stove in the corner.

The menu concentrates on homemade goodies: blueberry, chocolate chip, and applesauce muffins, apple spice cake, squares, and brownies, lemon bread, and banana bread. For group reservations, Hilda likes to make special pies. There are different kinds of black and herbal bagged teas, coffee, and cold drinks too. A specialty tea is one Hilda makes called horsetail tea—she picks and dries the leaves herself. Tea is served in a pot with a cup and saucer.

22-Birdwalk will also cater for murder mystery dinners, with decorating and cooking to suit the setting of the mystery. You can also hold business meetings or craft evenings and can choose a soup-and-sandwich-type meal or a more substantial lasagna. There is a disc golf course on the property that is open after hours and paid for by donation. If you book such an evening, the goodies and tea are available then also.

22-Birdwalk can also be booked for bus tours as it seats approximately forty people, and there are also picnic tables outside.

In the shop you can find John Stone's wildlife pictures, quilted work, crocheting and paper toile. There is always a cheery Christmas corner too. The aim of the tea house is to provide refreshment to both mind and body, and, at the same time, to maintain the beauty and peace of the country location.

22-Birdwalk Tea and Crafts
Between Caroline and Sundre, on the west side of Highway 22
T: (403) 722-3934 or 638-7356

Hours of Operation
June–August: 10:00 AM–6:00 PM daily
September–June: closed Tuesdays and Wednesdays

Parking: On site, free
Smoking: No
Wheelchair Accessible: Yes

Grandma *Bott's* Gift Shop and Tea Room ❦

You can *hear* the peace of this country spot. It may be a little off the beaten track, but the quiet and beauty of the beaver pond and surrounding trees are well worth the trip down a bit of gravel road. Since the tea house windows overlook the pond, you can enjoy your tea and the view. The building and the business, both six years old, were named in honour of Ray and Audrey Bott's grandmothers, who helped settle the area.

There's a soup of the day as well as sandwiches with home-made fillings, such as egg, chicken or seafood. For a bit of a change you might like to try tacos and antipasto, or tacos and a

spicy mustard "Zinger Dip." Then to finish off there are great desserts like Black Forest trifle, brownies, cookies, or the house specialty (and particularly worth the drive), homemade cheese-cakes with different fruit toppings. For the morning empty feeling, there are muffins too.

A variety of black and herbal teas is available, from Apricot to Queen Victoria. Tea is served in a ceramic pot with china cups and saucers. The coffee is good too, if that is your preference. Reservations are suggested for more than four people together.

The gift shop is a real delight, with many different choices to tempt you. Linens and curtains, china and glassware, bridal albums, pictures and frames are just a few of the items you will find. For the collector in the family, there are Matchbox collectibles and Coke and John Deere memorabilia. Murchie's teas and coffees are available for sale.

> *Wouldn't it be dreadful to live in a country where they didn't have tea?*
>
> — *Noel Coward*

Grandma Bott's Gift Shop and Tea Room
8 kilometres south of Highway 11 on Highway 22,
3 kilometres west at the sign
T: (403) 845-6221

Hours of Operation
Spring and Fall: Wednesday–Saturday 10:00 AM–5:00 PM
Sunday 2:00 PM–5:00 PM
July and August: 10:00 AM–5:00 PM daily
Closed Jan 1–May 1

Parking: On site, free
Smoking: No
Wheelchair Accessible: Yes

Timberline *T*ea and Coffee House ☙

The beamed ceiling, board-and-batten wainscoting, and warm gingham-clad walls welcome you as you walk in the door of the eighty-five-year-old house. It is a warm and rustic scheme that is evident even in the washrooms. There are French doors out to a patio for the nicer weather.

One of the house specialties is the homemade buns that accompany salads or other dishes. They are made fresh every day. If you are a cinnamon bun addict, you can find them fresh-made here on Mondays, Wednesdays, and Fridays.

There are lots of choices on the lunch menu including two homemade soups every day, a daily pasta special and another daily special. The salads are

particularly recommended, whether it's the grape and chicken, the Mexican chef's salad or the orange pecan romaine, all served with that fresh bun and low-fat dressings (also made on site). Some of the hot dishes are served with "cheesy potato wedges" that really add something special to your meal. Sandwiches and pitas are also on the menu. For the particularly health-conscious, there is a fruit and fibre plate.

Delicious desserts range from cookies and squares to pumpkin pie, mile-high lemon meringue pie, and Oreo cookie crumb cake, an ice cream dessert that is especially good on those hot days. The pièce de résistance is the Timberline Crunch, an ice cream pie made with crushed Skor bars.

Bagged teas, black and herbal, are arranged in a pretty basket for you to choose from and they are then served in ceramic teapots with cups and saucers. Two flavours of coffee, besides the Colombian and decaffeinated ones, are featured daily. All are made with freshly ground beans.

Friday evening is "Italian Buffet Night" which offers pasta and sauces, lasagna, salads, specialty breads and home-style desserts. Timberline does catering both on site and off. In the tea room, they can serve up to fifty people in several different rooms, and the patio can seat another twenty-seven.

The gift shop is upstairs in the former bedrooms of the house. You will find an extensive collection of local pottery and artwork, and other Canadian-made articles. There is china, glass-ware and woodwork too. If your buying preferences lean toward the edible, you can purchase the salad dressings and dips or the homemade buns. Pies and cinnamon buns are available for sale with one day's notice—well worth planning ahead.

Timberline Tea and Coffee House
5211 50th Street, Rocky Mountain House
T: (403) 845-2337

Hours of Operation
Summer: Monday–Saturday: 9:30 AM–4:00 PM for meals and desserts; 4:00–9:00 PM for desserts, ice cream, tea, and coffee
Winter: Monday–Saturday: 9:30 AM–4:00 PM
Friday 9:30 AM–9:00 PM

Parking: On site or on street, free
Smoking: No, except patio
Wheelchair Accessible: Yes, except gift shop

The *Grapevine* Tea House ❧

This tea house resides in an old house from the 1940s that was pulled onto the acreage some years ago. Rosella Brown and her husband and friends worked on it for two years before it was ready for its new use. They added a basement, a new veranda at the front, and a deck at the back that overlooks Trapper Creek. At one point they had to contend with a tree falling onto the roof and new veranda, but the house is now charmingly finished with plastered ceilings, lovely windows, and a fireplace. For those who enjoy renovation stories, this is a good one and Rosella has an album of pictures to go with it.

It's a light menu always including two soups: baked French onion and one other. With this you can have a variety of sandwiches, pitas or croissants, and there's also Caesar salad and garlic toast. Rosella is happy to make a grilled cheese sandwich for any children visiting. The homemade desserts are especially appealing—layered lemon dream squares and lemon meringue pie are both made with fresh lemons, or perhaps you would prefer a hot fudge brownie or strawberry shortcake with whipped cream. There are both loose teas and bagged herbals, all served in beautiful cups and saucers. Coffee and cold drinks are also available.

In December there are great Christmas specials: a mug of hot spiced cider, rich dark fruitcake, or Christmas pudding with caramel hard sauce and whipped cream.

The tea room seats only twelve inside and fifteen on the covered deck, so reservations are a good idea. Downstairs, beside the creek, there is a lovely bed and breakfast suite with two bedrooms and a complete kitchen. It is completely self-contained, but Rosella provides a continental breakfast to start the day properly. It is a lovely quiet spot and is open year-round.

Antiques and collectibles for sale are displayed throughout the main floor, veranda and bathroom included. There are pictures, mirrors, lamps, silk flower arrangements and willow furniture, and many more items tempting to the collector. When you step through the old screen door, you enter another, gentler era.

The Grapevine Tea House

Echo Canyon Estates, north of Rocky Mountain House, just off Highway 22
T: (403) 845-5456

Hours of Operation
May 1–December 30: Wednesday–Saturday 11:00 AM–5:00 PM
July and August: Wednesday–Sunday 11:00 AM–5:00 PM

Parking: On site, at top of stairs down to tea house
Smoking: No
Wheelchair Accessible: No

The *Parkland* and the Prairie

Ellis Bird Farm Tea House ☙

There is much to see and do at the Ellis Bird Farm, so it makes a good destination tea house. Brother and sister, Charlie and Winnie Ellis, fell in love with "their" birds in 1955 and spent their lives attracting and protecting different species. Their backyard became a haven for wildlife. When it was time for the Ellises to sell, they made an arrangement with Union Carbide to maintain the bird farm in perpetuity as a non-profit charitable organization.

The tea house itself is in the old Ellis farmhouse that was built in the early 1900s. There are the original built-in bookshelves that served as room dividers between the living and dining rooms, as well as a few pieces of the farmhouse furniture.

The menu is small but everything is freshly made in the farmhouse kitchen. There is always a daily special, perhaps mushroom soup or tuna sandwich and salad, as well as a "hearty luncheon feature" which could be a chicken Caesar with a cheese bun, or a soup and sandwich plate. A ham and cheese sandwich on a home-baked bun is always on the menu and there are plain peanut butter and jam or cheese sandwiches for younger people. There is a daily dessert feature (strawberry shortcake in season), as well as cinnamon buns, light cheesecake with saskatoon sauce, or the special "Birdsnest Scones" served with preserves and cream. There is also a Tea Time Special—the Birdsnest scone served with fresh fruit, cheese and a choice of beverage. A different twist on afternoon tea is called "Tea-Licious" and consists of a glass of Saskatoon cider followed by a tray of assorted home-baked dainties, fresh fruit and, of course, a pot of tea.

The popular house blend tea is Queen Mary, but there are other loose teas from which to choose, even a maple tea. All are served in teapots with old cups and saucers. Other special drinks are the non-alcoholic saskatoon berry cider or the Bluebird Quencher, a tangy rhubarb-based punch.

As an integral part of the tea room experience, you should visit the lovely gardens and walk some of the trails. The conservation message is a big part of the Ellis Bird Farm, and there is much to see. The Visitor Centre has interesting displays as well as items to buy: gardening paraphenalia, T-shirts, anything to do with birds, and particularly, unique bird houses. You might even get the chance to see the sheep, happily keeping the tea room lawn trimmed. Note: Cash is preferred.

Ellis Bird Farm Tea House
Southeast of Lacombe, on Prentiss Road
T: (403) 885-4477
www.ellisbirdfarm.ab.ca

Hours of Operation
May 20–September 2: Tuesday–Sunday and holidays
Mondays: 11:00 AM–5:00 PM

Parking: On site one quarter mile from Tea House
and Visitor Centre; closer for handicapped
Smoking: No
Wheelchair Accessible: Yes

Tea Time Special: $5.00, Tea-Licious: $6.00

Hulley's Hideaway

Big Valley is an intriguing little town that is going at things in a big way. Running off the main street is a Wild West-style mall that gives the impression that the local outlaw will be leaving his horse at the hitching post in front of any of the stores. There are great pictures of former days and historical plaques telling equally great stories. When I asked at the tea house about opening hours, I was told "8:00 in the morning as long as the trains are running." These are the trips from Stettler to Big Valley by steam train from May to October. You get to spend time in Big Valley, checking out the galleries and tea room and then chug back to Stettler—a lovely day out.

The menu on the blackboard changes daily. There are home-made soups and specials of roast chicken or roast beef, as well as "ham dinner." You can often find a buffalo cheeseburger or a number of salads—tossed salad with garlic toast, Greek salad, or chili taco salad. Soup and sandwich combinations are the most popular item, with a veggie and cream cheese sandwich for the vegetarian crew. A breakfast omelette is served all day.

Desserts and sweets include the Hulleys' famous cinnamon buns, every kind of pie from seasonal fruit pies to banana cream, lemon meringue, and super-rich sour cream raisin pie. There are also date squares and cookies.

Bagged teas of all kinds, black, green, and herbal, are all available, served in a teapot with a china cup and saucer. Regular and decaffeinated coffees are also available.

Neil and Vivian Hulley's paintings decorate the walls and are also for sale; bread, hamburger, hot dog and dinner buns are available, as are those famous cinnamon buns.

Train Information: All Aboard Railway Excursions
T: (403) 742-2811

Hulley's Hideaway
Main Street, Big Valley
T: (403) 876-2726

Hours of Operation
April through December: 8:00 AM–6:00 PM daily "as long as the trains are running"
December–March: Closed on Sundays

Parking: On street, free
Smoking: No
Wheelchair Accessible: Yes

*N*utcracker Sweet ☙

The Nutcracker Sweet started life as a collectible shop, with an emphasis on Christmas decorations. It was part of the collection of antique and collectible shops in Donalda, home of the giant lamp. Florence Walker soon discovered that visitors to the town also wanted a cup of tea and something good to eat, and the tea house grew rapidly. The building, on the main street of Donalda, was built in 1911 as a grocery and hardware store. It has been renovated but still looks the part and is very inviting. The little garden beside it provides the edible flowers on the desserts.

The lunch menu includes vegetable soup in a bread bowl,

Acapulco salad, pork tortilla and black bean chili. You can also choose a croissant with soup or a shrimp melt on sourdough bread. For desserts there are wonderful items such as blackberry or raspberry cheesecake, peach upside-down cake and a delicious cranberry cake with butter sauce. On hot days, ice creams are a favourite, too, whether in milkshakes, floats, or sundaes—especially with saskatoon berry sauce. The fresh fruit for these desserts all comes from the farmers' market in Ponoka, which is why Nutcracker Sweet is closed on Wednesdays, when Florence goes to choose her fruits and vegetables.

There are over twenty kinds of loose herbal and black teas to drink, as well as coffee and cold drinks. Teas are served in a nice pot with a cup and saucer.

In the shop you will still find collectibles, hand-made nut-crackers and other Christmas specialties, and many different kinds of fairies. You can also purchase Auntie Flo's bread and but-ter pickles and antipasto. After your visit to the Nutcracker Sweet you can wander over to the antique market, the lamp museum, the art gallery, and the historic creamery and finish up by taking pictures of the giant lamp at the centre of town.

Nutcracker Sweet
Main Street, Donalda
T: (403) 883-2888

Hours of Operation
May long weekend to Christmas Eve: 12:00 noon–5:30 PM, except Wednesdays

Parking: On street, free
Smoking: No
Wheelchair Accessible: No

Heart-Tea Lunch 🌱

Blaine, Lorena, and their daughter, Jill, were farmers who decided to have a career change and now operate the Heart-Tea Lunch Room and Heart's Delight Bed and Breakfast in Coronation. The house, built in the 1920s, had been vacant for three years when Blaine and Lorena bought it. It's a casual, down-home atmosphere in the charmingly renovated house with hardwood floors. There is also a pretty patio for use on sunny days. The two bed and breakfast rooms are upstairs under the sloping ceilings.

The menu changes daily but you will always find open-faced bun sandwiches and a choice of two soups with fresh biscuits.

There is a delicious broccoli salad with bacon, raisins and other, more secret, ingredients. The desserts are homemade carrot or poppyseed cake, chocolate cake with caramel sauce, and even a Skor cake. In the summer you will find strawberry shortcake, while warm gingerbread is for the cooler months.

Tea is served in individual pots, and since Blaine and Lorena know their customers, the ladies get cups and saucers and the men have their mugs. Herbal and black teas are available, as is coffee, including lattes.

The tea house is open later in the evenings for private dinners (two to twenty people), to celebrate anniversaries or talk business. The pictures on the walls are by a local artist and, besides decorating their present space, are for sale. Have a look at the bed and breakfast rooms upstairs if you can; you might want to book a little getaway and enjoy more of the home cooking.

> *My experience ... convinced me that tea was better than brandy, and during the last six months in Africa I took no brandy, even when sick taking tea instead.*
>
> *— Theodore Roosevelt, Letter, 1912*

Heart-Tea Lunch
5021 Norfolk Avenue, Coronation
T: (403) 578-4540

Hours of Operation
Monday–Saturday 11:30 AM–5:00 PM
Closed Christmas to New Year's

Parking: On street, free
Smoking: No, except on the patio
Wheelchair Accessible: Not yet, plans are in place

MacEachern Tea House ❦

Duncan MacEachern would undoubtedly have approved the use to which his house has been put for the last fourteen years. Mr. MacEachern, a businessman himself, was once mayor of Wetaskiwin and keenly supportive of businesses in the town. The house was built for him and his family in 1903 and was lived in by the family until the 1950s. It still has the lovely ambience of the older home with its old-fashioned wallpaper, wide wood trim and wooden chairs and tables. It seats thirty-two people comfortably, with room for another eighteen outside in good weather.

MacEachern Tea House is open for light breakfasts of

omelettes and cinnamon buns. Lunch is an extensive menu with daily specials—published every week in the local paper—and desserts of the week as well. Lois Walsh, the owner, does all her own shopping and cooking—no suppliers allowed, as she prefers to choose her own vegetables and fruit. Everything is made on the premises, including the salad dressings and the au jus for the beef dip. Many of the recipes have been handed down from owner to owner and are very much a part of the MacEachern tradition.

The specialty of the house is Lois's orange bun, an orange-flavoured cinnamon bun for which customers keep coming back. The buns are made fresh daily, so it's first come, first served, although if you call ahead you can get some to take home. MacEachern Tea House offers an evening dinner if booked in advance for ten people or more, and will also host anniversary parties and lunch meetings in an upstairs room.

There are over twenty varieties of loose tea on the menu as well as herbal teas by the bag. Homemade iced tea and lemonade are available, but for the die-hard coffee drinker, Lois blends her own coffees, which are also for sale. The tea house is fully licensed.

MacEachern Tea House
4719 50th Avenue, Wetaskiwin
T: (780) 352-8308

Hours of Operation
Monday–Friday 9:30 AM–4:00 PM
July and August Saturday 9:30 AM–4:00 PM
(Closed other Saturdays, all Sundays and Holidays)
Evening meals for ten or more by reservation only

Parking: Lot at rear of building or street parking in front, free
Smoking: No
Wheelchair accessible: No

Camrose *Railway Station*
Museum and Park ❧

The Camrose station was built in 1911 when it was the depot for the Canadian Northern Railway. While the occasional train does still trundle along the track, there are many more things to do than just wait at the station. Glenys and Bruce Smith have taken on what they call their "volunteer retirement job" of running the station as a tea room, museum, and whatever else they can think of.

The tea room can seat up to forty-two inside (that's a bus tour size) with room for more outside, weather permitting. Everything on the menu is homemade: several kinds of large muffins—including the special white chocolate apricot—cinnamon buns, and oatmeal chocolate chip and "Steam Train Gingerbread" cookies. The

kids can have fun "face" bunwiches if they are particularly hungry.

On Saturdays lunch is a themed feast; a particular province or a particular country may be featured. There are special days such as Ukrainian Day (in August) and Scandinavian Day, or you might find what Glenys calls a pioneer smorg, encompassing food from all pioneer groups around the turn of the century. The music matches each theme and Glenys does the research for everything during the winter months, planning menus and presentations. At Saturday lunches you can always find hot dogs for the kids too.

Many bagged teas are available, with a few suggestions on the menu as to relaxing or refreshing types. These are served in pots with cups and saucers. As well as special coffees, there is pink lemonade or peach drink for hot days.

There are lots of interesting things to do at the station, including riding the pumper car or watching the G-scale model railway in one of the beautiful themed gardens. You will also find the library and archives of the Canadian Northern Railway here.

It is a wonderful place for gardeners as well as railroad enthusiasts. Besides the garden railway, there is a hummingbird garden, a cottage garden, and one for the butterflies. A new vegetable garden is planned, to be kept as it would have been kept by the station master and his family.

Everything is done by dedicated volunteers, even the annual garden party in July with games, dancing, and live bands. During the winter months you can still book the tea room for special events, or, if you know any children in grade four, you might be able to sneak in with them to the program that takes them back to the early nineteen-hundreds. They get to wear the clothing of the time, work as members of the train crew, and cook and clean up their own lunch. Not a bad idea!

Camrose Railway Station Museum And Park
44th Street and 47th Avenue, Camrose
T: (780) 672-3099

Hours of Operation
Saturday of May long weekend to Saturday of September long weekend
Thursday and Friday: 1:00 PM–5:00 PM for tea and goodies
Saturday: 10:00 AM–5:00 PM for lunch and/or tea and goodies

Parking: On site, free
Smoking: No
Wheelchair accessible: Yes

The *Ruffington Tea Room* ☙

The Ruffington Tea Room is the first business to exist in this lovely old turn-of-the-century house; ten years ago it was still a private residence in the Historical District of Camrose. The owners have used the entire house for the tea room and gift shop, with each of the upstairs bedrooms having a slightly different theme in its items for sale. Even the upstairs bathroom is put to use with a display of personal care and luxury items.

The tea room is an old-fashioned garden-style room with trellis and flowers. If the weather is pleasant you can enjoy the same theme outside on the patio, and even the washroom is dec-

orated with a hand-painted sink and floral wallpaper.

There is a great menu to choose from, although the Ruffington is particularly well known for its cinnamon buns. For sandwiches there are such inspiring choices as a Higley Pigley (black forest ham, tomato, cucumber, and sprouts) and Chick's Delight (herbed egg salad topped with crisp lettuce). Full-sized salads are available, as are soups, quiche, quesadillas and pita pockets. The "Slice of Summer" on the menu means a different pie to try every week and there are scones and jam, carrot cake, muffins, and "today's flavour" of cheesecake.

Bagged tea, including herbal, is served in individual pots with china cups and saucers. Coffee is popular, especially lattes and flavoured cappuccinos. Cold drinks include lemonade, iced tea, and different flavours of Clearly Canadian sparkling water.

The Ruffington is happy to cater for birthday parties and other special occasions in the evenings and will also provide lunch for business meetings wherever you would like it delivered.

Because the gift shop is the entire upper floor, it has an extensive selection of pottery, florals, framed prints, woodwork and collectible Boyd and Ty bears. A great draw is the mouth-watering homemade fudge in every conceivable flavour.

The Ruffington Tea Room
4803 48th Street, Camrose
T: (780) 672-4500

Hours of Operation
Monday–Saturday 10:00 AM–5:30 PM (store)
10:00 AM–5:00 PM (tea room)
July and August: also open Sundays 11:30 AM–4:00 PM

Parking: On street, free
Smoking: No
Wheelchair accessible: No

$\mathscr{V}$alley Tea Room ☙

Stoney Creek valley is a lovely, peaceful spot to view while you are enjoying your lunch or tea at the Valley Tea Room. It's a little difficult to find, as from one side it looks as if it is part of the nearby campground, but once you are inside, the view through the large windows or from the deck takes over.

In the mornings you can indulge yourself with a home-baked jumbo muffin or a cheese omelette. At lunch the Valley's specialty is a California taco salad, but other salads, such as chicken Caesar or dill salad, are available too. There is always a quiche of the day as well as a Thai chicken wrap or a soft beef taco. For dessert the pies include Dutch apple or peach (depending on the season), a cream pie, saskatoon berry pie, or a specialty cake for that particular week. Coconut cream pie is a specialty of the

house, as is turtle cheesecake. There is a square-and-coffee treat for the morning or afternoon too. If you plan well and come for lunch on your birthday, you are awarded a "decadent dessert" to suit the occasion.

Twenty-seven bagged teas, black and herbal, are served in a warmed teapot with a cup and saucer. Coffee is also available, as are cold drinks with enticing names like Blueberry Bliss and Peach Passion.

The Valley Tea House happily caters to Christmas parties, and the raised hearth fireplace just adds to the Christmas cheer.

I got nasty habits; I take tea at three.
— Mick Jagger, "Live with Me"

Valley Tea Room
5230 39th Avenue, Camrose
T: (780) 672-3123

Hours of Operation
May long weekend to end of October: Tuesday–Saturday
10:30 AM–4:00 PM
November–May: Wednesday–Friday 11:00 AM–4:30 PM

Parking: On site, free
Smoking: No (except on terrace)
Wheelchair Accessible: Yes

Rosebush Craft and Tea House ❦

The Rosebush Craft and Tea House resides in a 1912 house and on a heritage farm. Karen and Ben Cole moved the house onto their farm four years ago, renovated, added a porch, and opened for business. The whole house, both upstairs and down, is beautifully decorated and filled with crafts and gifts.

The menu is seasonal and changes daily. Karen has found that her customers enjoy old-fashioned farm cooking, so that is what she prepares. There are always two homemade soups, one of them a cream soup. A specialty is chicken stew in a bread bowl,

or you can find a chicken Caesar salad. A salmon and sprouts croissant is a good choice but there are two or three other kinds of sandwiches too.

Desserts and sweets range from saskatoon berry torte to coconut cream pie and from chocolate cheesecake to cinnamon buns. There are over twenty varieties of bagged teas, black and herbal, served in teapots with a china cup and saucer. There are lots of coffees to try if you prefer.

The gift shop has a large selection of linens, candles, pictures, flower arrangements, dolls, and denim jackets. There are also rustic picture frames, baby gifts and a special Christmas room.

The tea house can seat twenty-four inside, twenty-four on the deck if the weather cooperates, and twenty-four more in a small barn renovated for the purpose. The small barn is also an important part of the Christmas open house, on the third weekend in November. It houses the crafters who come to display and sell their products as well as the poinsettias that are much in demand at that time of year. At the open house Karen serves Christmas cookies, apple cider and coffee. It's a special time and happily anticipated by those who have been in previous years.

Rosebush Craft and Tea House
Southwest of Camrose on Highway 56, three kilometres south of the Edberg Bridge
T: (780) 877-2243

Hours of Operation
May 1–Christmas: Tuesday–Saturday 11:00 AM–5:00 PM

Parking: On site, free
Smoking: No
Wheelchair Accessible: Yes

Tiny T-House ❧

It does look tiny but it operates in a big way. Tiny T-House seats about twenty-four people and, from the busy kitchen, Josephine Toews also operates "Out 2 Lunch," a take-out and delivery service that caters to a number of businesses in the area, including the local golf course. Both businesses are combined in a little eighty-year-old house just off the main street of Wainwright. Some catering of Christmas parties is part of the picture too.

The menu for the tea house includes two soups each day served with a homemade biscuit. Sandwiches are served on bread

or in pitas and can be egg, salmon, turkey, beef, ham, chicken salad, or vegetable. Soup and a half sandwich is a good choice too. If you're not in the mood for soup and sandwich, there are several "melts" available: ham and Swiss, tuna, or seafood. And if you are particularly hungry, you can have the daily special: on Mondays it's cheeseburgers, Tuesdays, lasagna served with Caesar salad and garlic toast, Wednesdays, chicken, Thursdays, farmer's sausage, and Fridays (surprise?), fish. Salads are also available.

For snacks there is a long list, beginning with the very popular cheese scones and including mini-loaves, muffins, or carrot cake. Other homemade desserts are cheesecake, pumpkin pie, or coconut cream pie and there is also a special dessert of the day— apple crisp, perhaps, or peach upside-down cake, depending on the season.

Teas are bagged, either black or herbal, served in a teapot with a cup and saucer. Coffee, iced tea, fruit juices and pop are also available.

Tiny T-House
917 4th Avenue, Wainwright
T: (780) 842-5767

Hours of Operation
Monday–Friday 11:00 AM–3:30 PM, closed holidays
Parking; On street, free

Smoking: Yes
Wheelchair Accessible: Yes

The *Galleria* ☙

The Galleria is a delightful step back into the waiting room of the old train station in Wainwright. There are still a few trains going through, but business for the train station these days is the bus service. Even on Christmas Day, Louella and Wally Komedina open their tea room when the buses come in, to offer travellers a cup of tea and a piece of pie.

On all the other days, there is an extensive lunch and tea time menu, starting with homemade soup and sandwiches, from egg salad to bacon, lettuce and tomato. The soup, sandwich and/or salad combinations are pretty popular here, but there are

other choices too. You could have a hot chicken Caesar, a smokie on a bun, a chicken or beef taco salad, or perhaps you would like a tropical fruit salad served with cottage cheese and a muffin. For the kids there are hot-dogs and jello jigglers.

The desserts and snacks are many and varied: cheesecakes, carrot cake, tarts, muffins, cinnamon buns and special scones and preserves. The pies are especially in demand: saskatoon, pecan, and the signature food of the Galleria, Louella's strawberry rhubarb pie.

Teas are bagged and the most in demand are Red Rose and Earl Grey. Herbal teas, coffee, hot chocolate, cappuccinos and café au lait are all available too.

When you have finished your visit to the tea room, you can step along the hall to the Wainwright Museum. There are eighteen rooms of historic displays and pioneer settings, so plan to spend some time looking around. The museum is open from 9:00 AM to 5:00 PM daily.

Come, let us have some tea and continue to talk about happy things.
— *Chaim Potok,* The Chosen

The Galleria
1001 1st Avenue, Wainwright
T: (780) 842-9166

Hours of Operation
9:00 AM–5:00 PM daily

Parking: On site, free
Smoking: There is a separate room for smokers
Wheelchair Accessible: Yes

The Gallery Tea House 🍃

Since the Gallery Tea House shares space with the Arts and Crafts society in Provost, you can book yourself into a class and then reward your hard work with tea and goodies. The Gallery is located in a small farmhouse that was moved into town many years ago. It remained a residence until the Arts and Crafts people purchased it and turned it into a gallery. Then came the tea room. There is plenty of space amidst the crafts for up to thirty people, including a private room that you can book for your own small party.

Besides the two homemade soups, there are daily features such as a filled croissant served with salad, a variety of chicken dishes,

or perhaps a lasagna. Take-out is available on these items too. The specialty of the Gallery tea house, though, is the dessert menu. The day I visited, the special was a butterscotch flapper pie but there was also angel food cake with strawberries and whipped cream, and lemon meringue pie. Other scrumptious desserts are strawberry swirl cheesecake, fresh fruit pies, squares, chocolate raspberry torte and the famous Skor cake. For a treat that's not quite so sweet, there are carrot, date, or blueberry muffins.

With any of these you still have to choose your favourite tea from a long list of bagged teas, including black, herbal, chai, and the particularly popular cranberry with its special health benefits. Tea is served in a teapot with a china cup and saucer. Flavoured coffees are available, and owner Laura Lakevold makes her own Swiss mocha and French vanilla. On hot days, Laura's homemade cranapple drink is much in demand.

The courses offered at the Arts and Crafts Gallery are listed in the community newspaper, but if you don't care to make your own, you can buy beautifully crafted items made by local crafters, often the very people who teach the courses. There are paintings, placemats, and potholders, as well as handmade greeting cards, paper toile pictures, and hand-painted stones for your garden or your desk. There are some beautifully decorated birdhouses and many other unique wood products such as garden benches, planters and quilt racks. It's a lovely place to do some shopping and then sit and relax with a pot of tea and one of Laura's tantalizing desserts.

The Gallery Tea House
5239 50th Street, Provost
T: (780) 753-2983

Hours of Operation
Tuesday–Friday 10:00 AM–4:30 PM

Parking: On site or on street, free
Smoking: No
Wheelchair Accessible: Yes

Marushka's Tea Room ❧

Marushka's Tea Room is in Maria Mykietyshyn's own home and is a charming room overlooking the deck and the back garden. In fact, in the summer months, you can have your tea served out on the deck if you prefer.

The tea room is open by reservation only and the stated hours are 2:00 to 4:00 in the afternoon. If you wish to book another time, Maria is very flexible and can probably accommodate you. There is a light afternoon tea consisting of scones with butter and homemade preserves, a dessert and a pot of tea. A slightly larger tea includes tea sandwiches as well. The dessert

could be a rhubarb custard pie, a fresh fruit crisp or compote, a chocolate cake or even a rice pudding, if that is your preference. All this can be arranged at time of reservation.

Maria also does special teas for special days. The Valentine's

Day tea is particularly attractive with its heart-shaped scones and heart-shaped shortbread, but there is also a Spring tea, a Mother's Day tea and a Harvest tea. For these events, there might be perogies, quiche, tea sandwiches, sometimes soups or salads, and always those great desserts. Everything is freshly made and many ingredients are from Maria's own garden. Marushka's is also open and a popular destination during the town-wide garage sale in the spring. The dates and times for the special events are advertised in the *Vegreville Observer*.

Tea is usually orange pekoe and coffee is also served. Maria also makes what she calls a "mulled tea," combining her homemade apple juice with Earl Grey tea for a different and delicious hot drink. All this is served at tables set with pretty linens and china.

Marushka's is also a bed and breakfast, and since Lavoy is only a few minutes from Vegreville, it makes an excellent place to stay if you are visiting the Pysanka or any of Vegreville's other Ukrainian specialties.

***

Marushka's Tea Room
5112 50th Street, Lavoy
T: (780) 658-2503

Hours of Operation
2:00 PM–4:00 PM; other hours as arranged

Parking: On street, free
Smoking: No
Wheelchair Accessible: No

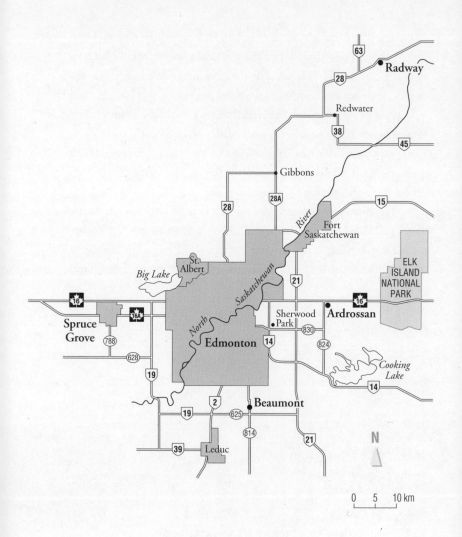

Edmonton and Area

Cargo and James

Cargo and James is a tea room in a modern setting. In the summer you can sit inside (with the doors open), or outside on the sidewalk, watching the world go by on Whyte Avenue. In the wintertime the gas fireplace is burning and there are comfortable couches and chairs to curl up in. Cargo and James has a huge selection of teas to choose from. Just check out the tea wall and select one from the 120 varieties. The staff are happy to explain the somewhat confusing differences in tea varieties, from the strictly herbal to black, green, or oolong. There is also good coffee available, and iced tea for hot days.

All the teas are for sale, whether in larger quantities or in lit-

tle gift bags or boxes, the latter being refillable if you want to try a different kind next time. There are also tea-related items such as different kinds of strainers for the loose tea, and tea pots, mugs and cups made by a local potter especially for Cargo and James.

Lunches consist of sandwiches on thick bread, including a vegetarian choice. There is also a fresh soup each day. If you want dessert or just a treat with your beverage, there are wonderful baked goods such as cinnamon twists, cinnamon stars, cookies, squares, and, of course, muffins and scones. Instead of one signature tea, Cargo and James has a special tea blend every week for you to try.

Cargo and James
10634 Whyte (82nd) Avenue, Edmonton
T: (780) 433-8152
www.cargoandjames.com

Hours of Operation
Monday–Thursday: 9:00 AM–10:00 PM
Friday–Sunday: 9:00 AM–11:00 PM

Parking: Meters in front or two-hour free parking on 83rd Avenue
Smoking: No
Wheelchair Accessible: Yes

Cargo and James has opened another location at City Centre West in Edmonton.

Cargo and James
City Centre West, 10200 102nd Avenue
T: (780) 425-3330
www.cargoandjames.com

Hours of Operation
Monday–Wednesday 6:00 AM–5:30 PM
Thursday and Friday 6:00 AM–9:00 PM
Saturday 10:00 AM–5:30 PM
Sunday 12:00 noon–5:30 PM

Smoking: No
Wheelchair Accessible: Yes

Steps the Urban Tea House ❦

The owners of Steeps the Urban Teahouse are tea purists; so that you won't be overwhelmed by the strong smell of coffee, they don't make it. There are over 160 varieties of loose tea to choose from so you probably won't miss the coffee. The teas have wonderful aromas of their own and are all stored in such a way that customers can make their choices based on appearance and an attractive aroma. Seventy-five percent of the teas are imported directly from Eastern Europe rather than through a North American wholesaler. The owners, brothers Brendan and Paul Waye, say that this makes the teas a bit more expensive but well

worth it, especially for the "basic" and most popular teas such as English breakfast, Irish breakfast and Earl Grey. If you want to know what new teas have arrived, you can access the Steeps website.

The most famous tea available at Steeps is their own chai tea. They actually have a company, Steeps Chai Ltd., that produces the chai concentrate and distributes it all over Canada. Chai lattes have become very popular and can be made with either milk or soy milk.

Baked goods such as cheese scones from a local bakery and heavenly pies from Edmonton's Twigs and Berries are much in demand. Although Steeps does not have a lunch menu as such, there is always a soup of the day to go with one of the cheese scones, as well as veggie or beef samosas to fill an empty spot.

The building dates from 1954. Deep-coloured walls with tea sayings and an interesting checkerboard floor create a serene atmosphere, while the mismatched wood tables and chairs add the serendipity touch. There is also a cozy corner with a loveseat and comfortable chairs. The high shelves are filled with old tea pots and tea canisters.

The chai concentrate is available for sale in four different flavours and you can buy any quantity of the loose teas. To help you make your best pot ever, Steeps also sells tea pots and all the latest tea-brewing devices.

A second location, Steeps Tea Lounge, can be found at: 11116 Whyte (82nd) Avenue, Edmonton.

Note: Steeps also has a Calgary location (see page 42).

Steeps the Urban Tea House
12411 Stony Plain Road, Edmonton
T: (780) 488-1505
www.steepstea.com

Hours of Operation
Monday–Thursday 9:00 AM–11:00 PM
Friday and Saturday 9:00 AM–12:00 midnight
Sunday 10:00 AM–11:00 PM

Parking: On street, metered
Smoking: No
Wheelchair accessible: Yes

$\mathcal{R}$utherford House ☞

Rutherford House was built by Alberta's first premier, A. C. Rutherford, as an elegant home in which to entertain important guests. It is hard to believe that this stately old house was due for demolition in the 1960s. Fortunately, a group of history enthusiasts was willing to spend the time and effort to form the Friends of Rutherford Society to restore the house and, eventually, to run it as a business.

Afternoon tea and other meals are served in the former Breakfast Room and the enclosed sunporch, although if the winter temperature drops too low for too long, the reception area and the sunporch have to switch functions.

The Rutherfords' house was completed in 1911, and, with the help of the late Hazel McCuaig (Premier Rutherford's daughter), it

has been restored to the year 1915. Pieces of furniture that were originally in the house have been found and sometimes donated, and many others that were appropriate to the period have been added. Mrs. Rutherford's piano is still in the front parlour where she often played it for friends or Ladies' Auxiliary functions. Tours of both floors of this beautiful house are available with guides in period costume or you can wander on your own after tea.

The Friends of Rutherford Society serves lunches, teas, high teas, and "just desserts." There are four afternoon teas to choose from, depending on how hungry you are. Lunches can be turkey or chicken dishes, baked red pepper Florentine or quiche (for the vegetarian diet), sandwiches, salads and "Soup of the Moment." Sandwiches are served on baguettes or Scottish baps. Desserts range from a Brie and fruit plate to a "Rutherford Sweet Ending," an assortment of Rutherford House goodies. The most popular lunch item is the Garneau sandwich, named after the area and made with poached chicken breast on a Scottish bap.

The gift shop, is an eclectic mix of tea accompaniments, linens, books, jewellery, and children's toys. There are also lunch and tour packages for groups, with various themes such as the restoration of the house, entertaining Edwardian style and wedding traditions and trousseaus. Rutherford House will also host weddings and other private receptions—a very special setting for very special events.

Signature tea blend: Rutherford House Blend (Buckingham Palace). Last seating is at 3:00 PM. Reservations are a good idea for lunch, required for groups for the tea and tour packages.

Rutherford House
11153 Saskatchewan Drive
T: (780) 427-4033

Hours of Operation
May 15–Labour Day: Tuesday–Sunday 12:00 noon–5:00 PM
Winter: Tuesday–Sunday 9:00 AM–5:00 PM

Parking: Nine free spaces on Saskatchewan Drive, meters also on Saskatchewan Drive or the university parking lot on 111th Street, just behind Rutherford House.
Smoking: No
Wheelchair Accessible: Yes

Rutherford  Afternoon Teas

Arbour High Tea
$15.00 for one, $28.00 for two
> Finger sandwiches, a savoury dish, sweet scones with raspberry butter, tea cakes, cookies, sweets, fresh fruit, and a pot of tea.

Mrs. Rutherford's Tea Plate
$11.00 for one, $21.00 for two
> Finger sandwiches, sweet scones with raspberry butter, tea cakes, cookies, sweets, fresh fruit, and tea.

Hazel's Tea Plate
$7.00 for one, $13.00 for two
> A sweet scone served with raspberry butter, decadent tea cakes, sweet squares and fruit, and tea.

Afternoon Scone Plate
$4.00 for one, $7.00 for two
> A sweet scone served with fruit and raspberry butter, and a pot of tea.

There are few hours in life more agreeable than the hour dedicated to the ceremony known as afternoon tea.
> — *Henry James, "The Portrait of a Lady."*

Fairmont Hotel MacDonald

The Fairmont Hotel MacDonald, which originally opened in 1915, is situated high on the banks of the North Saskatchewan River. The building was extensively renovated and restored to its former elegance in the early 1990s and is well worth a visit and a tour.

An elegant afternoon tea is served on Sunday afternoons in the lovely Harvest Room. Fruit cup begins the meal, followed by finger sandwiches, Victorian scones with Devonshire cream and strawberry jam, and a wonderful assortment of pastries and sweets. The tea, served in china teapots and cups and saucers, is the "Hotel MacDonald Special Blend," custom-blended by Edmonton's Fanta Camara.

Fairmont Hotel MacDonald
10065 100th Street, Edmonton
T: (780) 424-5181

Hours of Operation
May long weekend–September long weekend:
Sundays 3:00 PM–4:30 PM

Parking: Hotel parkade
Smoking: No
Wheelchair Accessible: Yes

Afternoon Tea: $22.95

ℳemories Tea House and Gift Boutique ☙

Memories are all over the place at Memories Tea House in Beaumont. Tea cups and saucers, plates and linens are on show throughout the tea room. Just outside the ladies' room there's a special vignette of Grandma's wedding dress and accessories, guarded by a large black and white photograph of the bride and groom on the wedding day.

The tea room is owned and operated by a mother and daughter team (daughter and granddaughter of the pictured bride and groom), who do all the cooking, baking and serving between

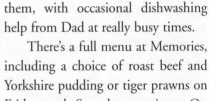

them, with occasional dishwashing help from Dad at really busy times.

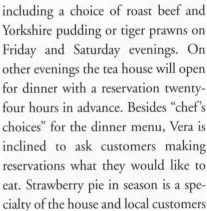

There's a full menu at Memories, including a choice of roast beef and Yorkshire pudding or tiger prawns on Friday and Saturday evenings. On other evenings the tea house will open for dinner with a reservation twenty-four hours in advance. Besides "chef's choices" for the dinner menu, Vera is inclined to ask customers making reservations what they would like to eat. Strawberry pie in season is a specialty of the house and local customers have been known to bring their own pie plate to take one home. Coconut cream pie is also in demand, but there are always six to eight desserts from which to choose. The restaurant is fully licensed. Reservations for lunch are a good idea, as large parties or bus tours can fill the tea room.

Memories offers high tea between two and four in the afternoon. It requires twenty-four hours notice as Vera insists that the

Devonshire cream be made properly. The high tea includes dainty sandwiches, mini-quiche and sausage rolls, tea biscuits, homemade jam, and Devonshire cream, all beautifully served.

The teas served at Memories are all loose tea blends ranging from English breakfast to bubblegum. The tea menu has very specific descriptions of each so you can decide what suits your tastebuds each time you visit.

Vera and Janna are happy to cater for any special occasions, birthdays, anniversaries, and meetings as well as the special requests of tour buses.

Memories has a gift shop in the tea room that features pictures, linens, china, and glassware as well as woodwork. Christmas begins in the tea room and the gift shop at the end of October with charming decorations and gifts for the season.

Note: Customers for evening meals should make reservations twenty-four hours in advance.

Memories Tea House and Gift Boutique
5001 50th Avenue, Beaumont
T: (780) 929-9029

Hours of Operation
Tuesday–Saturday 11:00 AM–6:00 PM

Parking: On site, free
Smoking: Permitted in a small area, although there is currently the possibility of town by-law being passed that will prohibit smoking in restaurants
Wheelchair accessible: Yes

High Tea: $14.95 per person

The Victorian Affair

For setting, this lovely old house takes the cake. The location just south of Spruce Grove puts it in the country, surrounded by beautiful old trees—on one of the days I visited, the trees were covered with hoarfrost and breathtakingly beautiful. The interior looks as if it has been preserved from the early 1900s—gently flowered wallpaper and masses of wood trim still with the original varnish finish. An old upright piano in the corner, a violin laid ready to play, and a large woodburning fireplace complete the picture.

The extensive menu includes appetizers such as shrimp in a garlic cream sauce and a Mediterranean platter for two that includes pita wedges, hummus, caviar spread and falafel. There are soup, stew and quiche specials every day as well as a vegetable or chicken rice bowl, a seafood melt and a chicken pesto on multigrain bread. Salads are a Victorian garden salad with raspberry vinaigrette dressing, a Danish cucumber salad or a Caesar salad with chicken.

The desserts, called "Sweet Endings," feature a torte of the day, brownie cake, and Cozonak, an Easter bread pudding. Nearly fifty teas are listed and described on the menu, from apple to Vienna Opera, and there is also the option of organic coffee.

High tea is served from 2:00 pm to 5:00 pm with advance reservations. It is served on the traditional three-tiered dish with scones, wonderful lemon curd and Devonshire cream, finger sandwiches and scrumptious "sweet stuff."

The Victorian Affair is fully licensed.

Tea! What greater thing is there than a proper cup of tea?!
— Anonymous

The Victorian Affair
Golden Spike Road (on the west side of the road, two kilometres south from Spruce Grove)
T: (780) 962-3177

Hours of Operation
Tuesday–Saturday 11:00 AM–9:00 PM
Sunday 11:00 AM–5:00 PM

Parking: On site, free
Smoking: No, except on veranda
Wheelchair Accessible: Yes

High tea: $23.00 for two, additional $12.95 per person

Strathcona Tea House ❧

The Strathcona Tea House is located in a beautiful old building that started life in 1906 as a branch of the Canadian Imperial Bank of Commerce in Vegreville. In 1992 the present owner, Marlhine Lothian, bought it and had it moved to its present location beside the antique and collectible shop that she had already been running for some years. Restored and renovated, the old bank now serves breakfasts, lunches and afternoon teas in a peaceful atmosphere, redolent of a quieter and gentler time.

Breakfast is served until 2:00 PM and offers bacon, sausage, or ham and eggs, or a Country Scramble that has mushrooms and cheese whipped into the eggs. Lunches include Caesar salads with either chicken or seafood, quiche, salmon steaks, and ostrich or bison patties. Liver and sautéed onions or a sirloin steak sandwich are there for a hearty appetite, or you might prefer a pork chop plate. Sandwiches are served on Anadama bread, the specialty of the house, renowned for its taste as well as its origin—a good story which you can read on the Strathcona's menu.

Strathcona has a large variety of teas, from English breakfast to chocolate mint, the latter smelling just like After Eight mints but without the calories. You can also have a herbal tea. All are served in a pot with a hand-knitted or crocheted tea cozy.

And then there are the goodies: desserts to choose from the tray, scones with homemade jam, and another specialty of the house, Welsh tea cakes, served with homemade jam and cream.

The tea house offers many other options. There are special parties for children's and young people's birthdays, tea leaf readings, and, once a month, a murder mystery dinner. If you're lucky you might also run into Harry, the resident ghost, who, like any good guest, flushes the toilet after use.

You can find antiques, collectibles, linens, gifts, and cards as well as a year-round selection of Christmas ornaments and treasures in the Treasure Chest next door. This building is original to the site and at one time was the school house. In both buildings, the staff are friendly and anxious to make your visit enjoyable.

Note: Reservations are a good idea, especially for lunch.

Strathcona Tea House
Wye Road and Range Road 221, Ardrossan
T: (780) 922-6963

Hours of Operation
Tuesday–Thursday 9:00 AM–3:00 PM
Friday–Saturday 9:00 AM–9:00 PM
Sunday 10:00 AM–7:00 PM
Open anytime for bookings of 15 or more
Closed most of January

Parking: On site, free
Smoking: No
Wheelchair Accessible: No

Country *Memories* Teahouse and Gifts ❧

This building was originally the Radway Robin Hood Flour building, built in 1919. In 1926 a residence was added at the back. The two together now house Country Memories Teahouse and Gifts. In the former commercial building, the old floors were carefully lifted and replaced after the rotting sub-floor had been repaired. The sales counter from the Robin Hood days still exists and now displays some of the collectibles in the store.

Breakfasts, lunches, and teas are served in the old commercial building and if you want a more formal atmosphere you can reserve one of the rooms in the former residence. They are all decorated individually and have a special feeling of an earlier era.

Breakfasts consist of skillet scrambles, pancakes or French toast, or a grilled breakfast melt. Continental breakfast is also

available. Lunches are hearty affairs, too, with two daily homemade soups to choose from, as well as sandwiches from egg salad to roast beef and onions. The day I visited, one of the soups had the intriguing name of Meatball Cowboy Soup. Salads include chicken Caesar, taco, a house salad, and a seafood house salad. You can follow up with a wrap or a chicken melt. A real special is the Ukrainian Delight consisting of—what else—pyrohy and kubasa.

Fresh baked breads and pastries are all part of the picture. Desserts include cherry pie, blueberry cobbler (very popular), chocolate fudge cake, and saskatoon pie. There are things like bread pudding, country caramel and raisin pudding, cheesecake with different toppings, cinnamon buns, cranberry pumpkin muffins, sour cream cinnamon loaf, and chocolate chip mini-loaves.

The gift area has many collectibles, floral arrangements, local arts and crafts, special plates, beautiful porcelain dolls, and baby and children's gifts. It is all decorated with old prints of local school pictures, sports teams and old buildings from the area. Even the placemats are laminated old newspapers and catalogue pages, so take time to read through yours.

It is obviously a favourite place for the people who live anywhere near Radway, but the guest books will show how many people have enjoyed their visit and have returned. It has a warm and welcoming atmosphere, and there's always the chance that someone will feel moved to perform on the old pump organ just to add to your experience.

Country Memories Teahouse and Gifts
One block west of Main Street, Radway
T: (780) 736-3900

Hours of Operation
Monday–Saturday 9:00 AM–5:00 PM
Sunday brunch 11:00 AM–2:00 PM
Wednesday, Thursday, Friday evenings by reservation
Closed January and February

Parking: On street, free
Smoking: No
Wheelchair Accessible: Yes

Afternoon Tea $9.50; High Tea $12.50 (24 hours advance notice required)

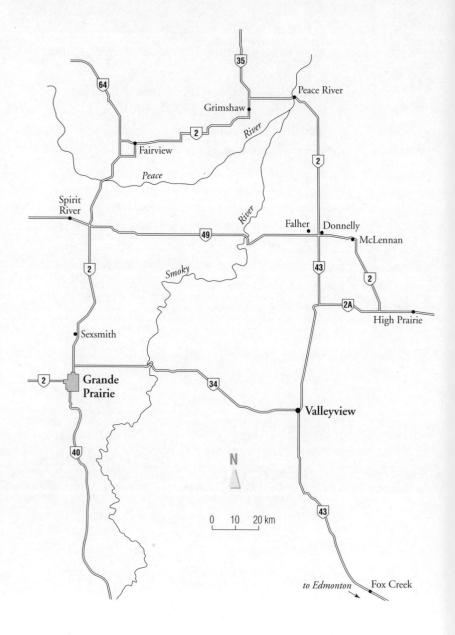

The *Peace*

$\mathcal{P}$inky's Tea House and Curio Shoppe ☙

Pinky's Tea House was in 1936 the first Catholic Church in Valleyview. Then it became a residence, and later still, a ladies' dress shop—somewhere in this chequered history, it was painted bright pink. Doreen and Bill Schram decided that it would make a great tea room for their property on the highway, so they arranged to move it. A five-thosand-dollar tab to move two wires on the road convinced Bill there was a better way. He sliced off the roof, covered what was left with a tarp, and went under the wires. The funny part of the story is that for some reason the house ended up on one side of the highway and the roof on the other. It all generated a great deal of laughter and lots of interest in the new venture.

When roof and walls were reunited, Doreen proceeded to decorate the main floor as the tea room and the upper floor as a bed

and breakfast. The tea room is charming and can seat thirty-two people, with several separate rooms that are very much in demand. Each table is beautifully set with different china and linen—blues, yellows, and blue and white in the main room, while pinks predominate in one of the smaller rooms. The more formal dining room is furnished and decorated with antiques.

Everything is done by reservation at Pinky's and it is one of the few tea rooms that does an actual high tea. That includes chicken pot pie, biscuits, clotted cream and homemade jam, and little pastries and cakes. If you can't manage high tea, you can still have tea and homemade cakes, tarts, pies or Swedish pastry.

Lunches are fine feasts. A popular one is chicken in puff pastry, served with salad, hot vegetables, homemade biscuit, dessert and beverage. There are other chicken recipes as well as a mini-meatloaf, gourmet potatoes, vegetables and gravy. If a reservation is for more than four people, Doreen will make you roast beef or pork loin roast with all the accompaniments. Quiche is another possibility, and, if you are the first one calling for a reservation on a particular day, you can help choose the menu!

Dinner is available, often a larger version of the lunch choices. One of the most popular dinners is Cornish game hens with burgundy sauce and wild rice stuffing.

The Curio Shoppe is in a separate building and features antiques and collectibles of all sorts, as well as some locally made embroidered and quilted goods. Pinky's is a delightful place to visit, and, if you get a glimpse of the bed and breakfast rooms, you'll want to have a sleepover.

Pinky's Tea House and Curio Shoppe
Thirteen miles west of Valleyview on the south side of Highway 43
T: (780) 524-2412

Hours of Operation
Lunch: 12:00 noon–2:00 PM; Teas: 1:00 PM–4:00 PM
Dinner: From 5:30 PM

Parking: On site, free
Smoking: No
Wheelchair Accessible: Yes

High Tea: $15.00

The Old Barn Store and Tea House ❧

There's a store, a greenhouse operation, and a tea house at Dunvegan Gardens, so it makes a great outing. The greenhouse operation deals with "all your gardening and landscape needs," the store has everything you could want from china to clothing, and the tea house will serve you lunch or treats (or both) in a charming setting.

Lunch can be a hearty lasagna, chicken pot pie, fish and chips, a hamburger, or hot wings. If you prefer something a little lighter there is a chicken breast sandwich, chicken quesadillas, or a Caesar salad. Another option would be a bowl of soup and a

scone, croissant, or johnnycake. Everything is made on site and some things (like the chicken pot pie) take a little longer in order to taste just right.

Besides the scones and johnnycake, there's a large variety of desserts: pies, cheesecakes, German chocolate cake, strawberry shortcake, or, for a really hot day, an ice cream sundae. Another hot day refreshment is a raspberry- or saskatoon-berry- flavoured lemonade. There are over twenty-five varieties of loose and bagged teas, including herbals, and there is coffee to drink if you prefer.

Dunvegan Gardens (the gardening and landscaping business) was begun in 1977 and the tea room added in 1995. The old barn is the present sales building and the tea room and gift shop are in the new barn and silo combination. The tea room, which seats fifty people, is beautifully decorated with rose wallpaper, and the tables are surrounded by the lovely displays of goods for sale. You can find pottery, antiques, linens, fine china, pictures, stuffies, and ladies' clothing. There's even a pretty display at the top of a winding stair in the silo.

The Old Barn Store and Tea House
Three kilometres south of 84th Avenue, on
Highway 40, Grande Prairie
T: (780) 532-3212

Hours of Operation
Monday–Saturday 10:00 AM–5:00 PM
Usually closed on holidays and Sundays

Parking: On site, free
Smoking: No
Wheelchair Accessible: No

Recipes, Retailers and *More* About Tea

Recipes

Pumpkin Bars
McCracken Country Inn, Hinton

>   4 eggs
>   1 cup oil
>   2 cups sugar
>   1 15 oz can pumpkin

Mix together.

>   2 cups flour
>   2 tsp baking powder
>   ½ tsp salt
>   1 tsp baking soda
>   2 tsp cinnamon
>   ½ tsp ginger
>   ½ tsp cloves
>   ½ tsp nutmeg

Mix these dry ingredients together. Add pumpkin mixture and mix well. Pour mixture into large greased cookie sheet: 10 by 15 inch. Bake at 350 degrees for 25–30 minutes. Ice when cool.

Icing
>   4 oz cream cheese
>   2 tbsp butter
>   1 tbsp cream
>   1 tsp vanilla
>   3 cups icing sugar

Beat cream cheese, butter, vanilla and cream. Add icing sugar, beat until creamy. Spread on bars.

These bars can be frozen.

Doreen's Biscuits
Pinky's Tea House, Valleyview

> 2 cups flour
> ½ tsp sugar
> ⅛ tsp salt
> 1 ½ tbsp baking powder
> 1 cup milk
> ¼ cup oil
> 1 large egg

Mix dry ingredients really well. Beat liquid ingredients together. Fold gently into dry mixture. Place in greased muffin tins. Bake at 350 degrees for 25 minutes. These are also good with herbs or cheese added, depending on what they are being served with.

Lavender Mint Iced Tea
Jasmine Tea Room, Lethbridge

> 6 tsps Moonlight Lavender tea leaves
>   (or another lavender-mint blend)
> ¾ cup sugar
> ¾ cup lemon juice
> 6 cups boiling water
> 2 cups cold water

Brew the lavender tea in 6 cups boiled water (half an hour brewing time at least). Cool slightly; pour into jug. Add sugar and stir to dissolve. Add lemon juice and cold water. Serve over ice. Garnish with lemon slice or sprig of mint. Makes 8 cups.

Light Delight Cheesecake
Ellis Bird Farm, Lacombe

Crust

    2 cups graham wafer crumbs

    ¼ cup margarine

    2 tbsps sugar

Cake

    3-oz. package of Jello

    1 cup hot water

    1 cup whipping cream

    8 oz cream cheese softened

    ⅔ cup sugar

    2 tsps vanilla

Put crust in a large springform cheesecake pan and bake at 350 degrees for 10 minutes.

Dissolve Jello in water and cool until it begins to thicken. Whip cream and set it aside. Mix cream cheese with the thickened Jello. Add sugar and vanilla. Beat mixture until smooth. Fold in the whipped cream. Pour over the crust and chill. Top with your favourite fruit sauce—saskatoon berry is delicious.

Tea is drunk to forget the din of the world.

                        — T'ien Yiheng

Brown Sugar Sauce
Heart-Tea Lunch, Coronation

> ½ cup butter
> 1 cup whipping cream
> 1 cup brown sugar

Bring to boil and serve warm over light cake.

Blueberry Poppins Muffins
Country Memories, Radway

Muffins
> 2 cups flour
> 2 tsp baking powder
> 1 tsp salt
> 1 cup sugar
> 1 ½ cups blueberries
> ¼ cup melted butter
> 1 cup milk
> 2 eggs

Topping
> ½ cup flour
> ¼ tsp cinnamon
> ¼ tsp salt
> ¾ cup brown sugar
> ¼ cup butter

Mix dry ingredients and stir in milk, melted butter, eggs and blueberries. Fill cupcake pans ¾ full. Sprinkle with topping mixture and bake at 350 degrees for 20–25 minutes.

Mother's Fruit Torte
Mother Mountain, Delia

Pastry
> 2 cups flour
> ¼ cup sugar
> 1 cup butter
> 2 egg yolks

Mix flour and sugar. Cut in butter until mixture resembles coarse crumbs. Add egg yolks to form dough. Press into 10-inch spring-form pan, making sure dough comes up ½ inch on sides of pan. Bake in preheated 375 degree oven for 25 minutes.

Filling
> 3 to 4 cups fresh, frozen or canned fruit (add ½ cup sugar
>   and ¼ cup water if using fresh fruit)
> 2 tbsps cornstarch

Drain canned or frozen fruit, reserve juice and add water to make one cup. Mix cornstarch and fruit juices, cook until thickened. Place fruit in pastry shell and pour thickened juice mixture over top. Chill. Remove carefully from pan. Serve with fresh whipped cream.

White Chocolate Apricot Muffins
Camrose Railway Station, Camrose

3 ½ cups all purpose flour
1 cup sugar
2 tbsps minced crystallized ginger
3 tsps baking powder
1 tsp salt
4 oz white baking chocolate, cut fine
1 ½ cups low-fat milk
6 tbsps melted margarine
2 large eggs, lightly beaten
1 cup apricot preserves
2 tbsps sugar

Preheat oven to 350 degrees.

Lightly spoon flour into dry measuring cup, level with a knife.

Combine flour and the next 5 ingredients (flour through chocolate) in a large bowl. Stir well with a whisk. Make a well in the centre of mixture. Combine milk, butter and egg and stir with whisk. Add to flour mixture just until moist. Put half of batter into muffin tins. Spoon 2 tsps of preserves into the centre of each muffin cup (do not spread over batter). Top with remaining batter. Sprinkle evenly with sugar.

Bake for about 22 minutes or until muffins spring back lightly when touched. Turn around halfway through. Remove from pan and cool completely. Makes 18 extra-large muffins (199 calories each).

Vera's Fresh Strawberry Pie
Memories, Beaumont

1 baked pie crust not pricked
Icing sugar to sprinkle over pie crust
4 cups fresh strawberries
1 cup sugar
3 ½ tbsps corn starch
1 tbsp lemon juice

Sprinkle icing sugar over pie shell. Pick over the berries, taking out 2 cups of whole, nicely shaped berries. Put the whole best berries into the bottom of the pie shell, pointy ends up. Arrange in circles or some kind of pleasing pattern.

Coarsely chop the remaining berries into a small saucepan. Mix sugar and cornstarch together and add to the chopped berries, cooking slowly until mixture is thick and clear. Remove from heat and add lemon juice. Pour sauce over the berries in the pie shell. Chill. Top with whipped cream, fresh berry and a mint sprig.

Come along inside ... We'll see if tea and buns can make the world a better place.

— Kenneth Grahame

Ruffington Blueberry Muffins
The Ruffington, Camrose

5 cups flour
1 ½ cups sugar
4 tsps baking powder
1 tsp salt
1 cup margarine.
2 cups blueberry yogurt
4 eggs
1 tsp almond flavouring

Mix together first four ingredients. Cut in margarine. Mix in yogurt, eggs, and almond flavouring. Do not overmix. Fold in 2 cups fresh or frozen blueberries. Fill greased muffin tins ¾ full. Bake at 350 degrees for 20–25 minutes. Makes 16 muffins.

Mrs. Rutherford's Traditional Shortbread
Rutherford Tea Room, Edmonton

1 ½ cups icing sugar
4 tbsps cornstarch
4 cups flour
1 lb soft, unsalted butter
½ tsp almond flavouring
Red and green cherries (optional)

Sift dry ingredients. Cut in butter and knead until mixture holds together. Roll on lightly floured surface to ⅛ inch thickness. Cut into various shapes, place on ungreased cookie sheet and decorate with cherries. Bake at 350 degrees for 10–12 minutes. Remove from pan and allow to cool on racks. Yield: 5 dozen cookies.

Herbed Beer Bread
Memories, Beaumont

2 ¾ cups flour
2 tbsps sugar
2 tbsps baking powder
1 tsp salt
¼ tsp oregano
¼ tsp thyme
¼ tsp dried dill weed
12-oz can beer

In a large bowl, stir the first seven ingredients. Add beer and mix well.

Place batter in a 4 by 8 greased loaf pan. Bake at 375 degrees for 50 minutes, or until golden on top. Brush the top with butter. Let stand in pan for 5 minutes before turning onto a cooling rack. Yield: One loaf.

Note: Beer bread makes a nice gift from your kitchen. Place the first 7 ingredients in an airtight container. Include the bottle of beer and directions for baking.

Mocha Revel Cake
That Country Place, Hanna

    1 cup brown sugar
    ½ cup flour
    ⅓ cup cocoa
    ¼ cup butter/margarine

Mix until crumbly and set aside.

Blend together:
    3 eggs
    1 yellow cake mix
    1 ¼ cups water
    ¼ cup oil
    1 tbsp instant coffee

Pour half the batter into a well greased bundt pan, sprinkle with half of the cocoa mixture, followed by remaining batter, then remainder of cocoa mixture. Bake at 350 degrees for 30 minutes. This is great with ice cream and chocolate or caramel sauce. Top with shaved chocolate.

Cabbage Roll Soup
Damon Lanes, Medicine Hat

1 lb ground beef
1 medium onion
1 tsp crushed garlic
1 14-oz can diced tomatoes
½ tsp sage
½ tsp ground pepper
1 tsp salt
8 cups water
1 10-oz can consomme
2 cups cabbage, shredded
½ cup uncooked rice

Brown beef and drain. Add onions and garlic and fry until onion starts to soften. Add tomatoes, seasonings, water, consomme and cabbage. Simmer 1 ½ hours until cabbage is tender. Add rice and cook an additional ½ hour. Adjust salt if necessary. Freezes well. Serves eight.

Miner's Lunch
Willow Tea Room, East Coulee

Garlic sausage and cheese on brown bread (mayo as desired).

Serve with onions, sauerkraut and a pickle. No coal dust necessary.

About Tea ✍

Types of Tea

Teas are categorized based on the method of their production. They all come from the same basic plant, but after the leaves are picked, they are treated differently to produce black, green or oolong teas. For black teas, the leaves are fermented first while for green teas, the leaves are heat-treated to kill enzymes that would allow the tea to oxidize or ferment. Oolong is somewhere in the middle. Its leaves have to be picked at a very precise time and are only partially fermented. White tea is a very special and expensive tea that is grown only high up in the Chinese mountains.

Teas of any kind can then be flavoured with fruits, flowers, herbs or spices and can also be mixed together to produce your favourite blend. Blends are just what the name implies and include such things as Earl Grey, a bergamot-flavoured black tea, or English Breakfast, usually containing an Assam tea, Ceylon tea and probably one from Kenya, all depending on the particular blending company.

Herbal teas, or tisanes, are not teas at all, but are made from other plants such as camomile and peppermint. Rooibos "teas" from South Africa are made from a type of cedar tree and have become quite well-known in North America.

Different types of tea and herbal tisanes are thought to be aids to health. Peppermint tea is supposed to be particularly good for digestion, while Rooibos enthusiasts say it is good for preventing and treating prostate cancer. Recent research is supporting the idea that tea can prevent some cancers, heart disease and strokes. I recommended Rooibos tea to a friend with prostate cancer and his response was, "How can anything that tastes that good have medicinal properties?"

Brewing Methods

One of the key ingredients for good tea is cold, fresh water brought to a full boil. Warm the pot with some of the nearly boiling water, empty it out, add the tea or tea bag(s) and pour on the boiling water. Steeping time varies for different kinds of tea but five minutes is a good starting point until you work out how strong you like that particular tea. Some people leave the tea leaves or bags in the pot for the second cup, others take it out and just keep the pot warm for the next cup.

Tea Pots and Accessories

Tea pots come in all shapes, sizes and styles—they even make really cute tea pots that you can't make tea in, so make sure the one you're considering is the real thing. The brown betty is the old-fashioned and still popular choice, while aluminum pots have become suspect because of possible links between aluminum and Alzheimer's disease. China pots make good tea and look elegant while pottery pots make good tea and look warm and comforting.

The French press has become popular in the more sophisticated tea rooms. It is a glass pot with a built-in diffuser or strainer that sits at the top of the pot until the tea is steeped. You then push the diffuser down to the bottom of the pot and pour your tea.

There are many things available to help you enjoy the tea experience. Tea cozies are an excellent idea for keeping the pot warm and they come in a huge variety of different styles. Some go right over the whole pot including its handle and spout (handles can get hot in there, so be careful), and some have holes for the handle and the spout. They can be crocheted, knitted or sewn from beautiful padded fabrics, while some are made of copper and fit snugly over the pot.

Loose tea requires some kind of receptacle in the pot or you end up with bits of tea leaves in your cup and a mass of wet tea leaves when you empty the pot. There are tea balls that are put right into the tea pot as well as diffusers shaped like cups that sit in the top of the pot while you pour the water over them. Some tea pots are designed with their own diffusers so that you can measure the tea right into them—very convenient. There are also paper tea filters that you fill and hang on the side of your teapot. After the tea is steeped or you have finished all the tea, you can just lift out the sack and put it in the compost.

Old-fashioned tea strainers, usually silver, are long-handled strainers that you put on the cup as you pour out the tea, especially important for loose teas that have not been contained in a tea ball or bag.

What you drink your tea in is entirely up to you. Some people like a nice thick mug while others insist on a china cup and saucer. I enjoy either, depending on the time of the day and the outside temperature! Curling up in a big armchair with a nice mug of hot tea is a great winter experience, while entertaining a friend with my best cups and saucers and china pot is particularly nice in the spring or summer.

Other Interesting Things to Do With Tea ✎

✦ Smoke salmon with it—Crazyweed Kitchen in Canmore serves and sells it.

>   2–626 Main Street
>   T: (403) 609-2530

✦ Make ice cream with it—green tea ice cream is available in most grocery stores and many restaurants.

✦ Make tea out of popped rice—maybe you should sample it first at Acquired Tastes in Edmonton (page 138).

✦ Smoke duck with it—try tea-smoked duck at the River Café in Calgary.

>   Prince's Island Park
>   T: (403) 261-7670
>   www.river-cafe.com

✦ Go teenage and try it in a slush—Cargo and James in Edmonton (page 98) will oblige.

✦ Wash your face in *extremely* well-steeped Rooibos—it's great for the complexion and my 16-year-old daughter swears by it.

Bubble Tea Hotline ☞

Stop the presses! I thought you might like to know the latest tea trend: bubble tea—also called Boba tea or tapioca milk tea.

It's usually served cold and it's shaken like a cocktail. It has a variety of ingredients; one of them is tea, and others may include honey and melon, banana and barley germ, or hundreds of other flavour combinations. The main ingredient that distinguishes this drink is sago: tapioca pearls, made from tapioca starches and sweet potatoes.

There are a few bubble tea places in Edmonton and Calgary, very often associated with Chinatown (the movement began in Taiwan). Other outlets will likely spring up, perhaps even in smaller cities and towns across the province, as bubble tea catches on. The trend is new and so are the cafés. I have listed the ones I have found and will let you call for their hours of operation.

Edmonton

Boba Planet
10750 82nd (Whyte) Ave
T: (780) 489-0089
www.bobaplanet.net

The Tea Cottage
10588 100 St
T: (780) 425-6404

The Tea Bar Café
10640 98 St
T: (780) 424-0696

Calgary

Dessert Dynasty
139–328 Centre St SE
(Dragon City Mall)
T: (403) 264-8888

Ten Ren Tea & Ginseng Co.
800F–999 36th St NE
T: (403) 207-8888

Tea Retailers 🌿

These shops carry many varieties of tea for sale, and some of them carry tea-related items such as tea-making accessories and tea-related gifts. Call or visit their web sites for more information.

Calgary

Lavendar Cove Tea & Gifts
210–5111 Northland Dr NW
(Northland Village Mall)
T: (403) 247-1177
www.teas-online.com

Shinng Tea Specialty
T: (403) 278-3182
www.shinngtea.com

Tea Affair
T: (403) 228-3635 /
(866) 832-7467 (toll-free)
www.tea-affair.com

Tea & Collection
192–1623 Centre St NW
(Central Landmark Mall)
T: (403) 276-7778

Tea Trader
6–1922 9th Ave SE
T: (403) 264-0728 /
(888) 676-2939 (toll-free)
www.teatrader.com

Ten Ren Tea & Ginseng Co
800F–999 36th St NE
T: (403) 207-8888

Edmonton

Acquired Tastes Tea Co
12516 102nd Ave
T: (780) 414-6041
www.canadiantea.com

Sino Tea Specialties
15525 Stony Plain Rd
T: (780) 486-1136

Lethbridge

Cupper's Coffee & Tea
912 1st Ave S
T: (403) 380-4555

Gatherings Tea ❦

From their headquarters in Devon, Wendy and Wes Whitbeck sell tea through a party system, hosting small parties in private homes and large ones for church groups. Representatives in different areas help people host tea parties where the group can sample different teas, play tea games, try out the latest tea accessories, eat some goodies and generally have a good time.

The Whitbecks, who once lived on Earl Grey Street and should have seen what was coming, started Gatherings Tea after a large family Thanksgiving dinner, where the general consensus was that "you can't get good tea anymore." After a lot of research and sampling, they decided to go into business distributing good quality teas and they haven't looked back.

The Whitbecks do most of their advertising on the web and they have a terrific catalogue outlining all the products available. There's a huge variety of teas, and new ones coming all the time. This summer they are adding an Inuit herbal tea, and, because of the high demand, an instant Chai tea.

"People are becoming more and more interested in what they can do about their health," says Wendy, "so tea fits well with that interest." Whether it's the general benefits of any black tea or the specific purposes in drinking Rooibos, they are aware that tea has a lot of advantages over "that other beverage."

T: (780) 999-4177 • F: (780) 987-5734 • www.gatheringstea.com

A Tip of the Teacup To ❧

❧ Victorian Affair in Spruce Grove for the most beautiful winter setting.

❧ Rutherford House in Edmonton for the most fascinating history.

❧ Steeps in Calgary for the most sophisticated décor.

❧ Grandma Bott's near Rocky Mountain House for the most peaceful setting.

❧ Pinky's in Valleyview for the prettiest table settings.

❧ Lake Agnes and Plain of Six Glaciers—"up" from Lake Louise—tied for the most breathtaking views and the most difficult to arrive at.

❧ The Grapevine Tea House near Rocky Mountain House for a lovely display of antiques.

❧ Camrose Railway Station for the best use of a train station (since we don't seem to have many trains that need stations any more).

❧ From the Prairie in Brooks for being the most like the neighbourhood pub, without the alcohol.

❧ That Country Place in Hanna for its lovely bed and breakfast under the eaves.

❧ Jasmine Tea Room in Lethbridge for the most comfortable chairs.

❧ That's Crafty for the best use of an old barn.

❧ Country Memories in Radway for the friendliest atmosphere—people shared coffee pots and poured for each other!

❧ MacEachern House in Wetaskiwin for celebrating the 100th anniversary of the old house this year.

❧ 22-Birdwalk near Sundre for its outdoor activities.

❧ Cargo and James in Edmonton for the best selection of teas to take home.

❧ And for me, the overall favourite, Pinky's in Valleyview for the great renovation story, the super food beautifully served, and the absolutely charming bed and breakfast where my daughter and I and our French exchange student were so warmly welcomed on an extremely cold and foggy night in November.

Tea and books—Mmmmmm, two of life's exquisite pleasures that together bring near-bliss.
— Christine Hanrahan

Lists 🌱

Afternoon / High Tea
Conversations Tea Room, 46
Country Memories, (by
    request only) 112
Ellis Bird Farm, 70
Fairmont Banff Springs Hotel,
    29
Fairmont Hotel MacDonald,
    105
Home Quarter, 52
Jasmine Room, 2
McCracken, 36
Memories, 106
Pinky's, 116
Prince of Wales Hotel, 28
Rutherford House, 102
Tara's Treasures, 48
Tea and Time, 44
Victorian Affair, 108
Yorkshire Rose (by request
    only), 6

Breakfast
Conversations, 46
Country Memories, 112
Doll Palace, 22
Home Quarter, 52
Hulley's Hideaway, 72
MacEachern, 78
Maligne Canyon, 38
McCracken, 36
Saskatoon Farm, 50
Strathcona, 110
Tara's Treasures, 48

Tea and Time, 44
Valley, 84
Willow, 18

Lunch
Camrose Railway Station
    (Saturday only), 80
Cargo and James, 98
Conversations, 46
Country Memories, 112
Damon Lanes, 4
Doll Palace, 22
Ellis Bird Farm, 70
Galleria, 90
Gallery, 92
Grandma Bott's, 62
Grapevine, 66
Heart-Tea Lunch, 76
Home Quarter, 52
Hulley's Hideaway, 72
Jasmine Room, 2
Lake Agnes, 30
MacEachern, 78
Maligne Canyon, 38
McCracken, 36
Memories, 106
Mother Mountain, 20
Murray House, 14
Nutcracker Sweet, 74
Old Barn Store, 118
PaSu Farm, 56
Pinky's, 116
Plain of Six Glaciers, 32
Prairie Elevator, 8

Rosebush, 86
Ruffington, 82
Rutherford House, 102
Saskatoon Farm, 50
Steeps, Calgary, 42
Strathcona, 110
Tara's Treasures, 48
Tea and Time, 44
Tea Cozy, 58
That Country Place, 24
That's Crafty, 12
Timberline, 64
Tiny T-House, 88
Valley, 84
Victorian Affair, 108
Whistling Kettle, 16
Willow, 18
Yorkshire Rose, 6

Dinner

Country Memories (by reservation only), 112
Heart-Tea Lunch (by reservation only), 76
Home Quarter, 52
MacEachern (by reservation only), 78
Maligne Canyon, 38
Memories, 106
Mother Mountain, 20
PaSu Farm, 56
Pinky's, 116
Timberline (Friday only), 64
Victorian Affair, 108

Special Occasions / Large Parties

22-Birdwalk, 60
Camrose Railway Station, 80
Conversations, 46
Damon Lanes, 4
Marushka's, 94
MacEachern, 78
McCracken, 36
Mother Mountain, 20
PaSu Farm, 56
Rosebush, 86
Strathcona, 110
That Country Place, 24
Yorkshire Rose, 6

Bed & Breakfast

Grapevine, 66
Heart-Tea Lunch, 76
Marushka's, 94
McCracken, 36
Pinky's, 116
That Country Place, 24

Catering

Conversations, 46
Damon Lanes, 4
Memories, 106
PaSu, 56
Ruffington, 82
Timberline, 64
Tiny T-House, 88
Valley, 84
Yorkshire Rose, 6

Alphabetical Listing of Tea Houses 🌿

MARY OAKWELL was born in Surrey, England and emigrated to Canada in 1957. She has been working on a variety of writing projects and most recently has published articles in Westjet's *Airlines* magazine.

When she's not drinking tea or writing, she can be found at the top of a ladder with hammer or paintbrush in hand, renovating the current home—at present in the Old Strathcona district of Edmonton where she lives with her 16-year-old daughter and two cats.

CELEBRATE ALBERTA!

Packed pantry-full of information
on Alberta's dynamic food scene,
*The Food Lover's Trail Guide to
Alberta* will make even the armchair
traveller hungry for the road. This
book is the mother lode of appetiz-
ing information about how to find:

- the best food
- the producers
- restaurants and chefs
- the bakers, the sausage makers
- the specialty grocers
- farmers' markets, U-picks . . .

Find out where good cooks shop in Medicine Hat, who stocks
the best candy in Calgary, how to find great traditional cheese in
Lacombe, and what's baking in Edmonton. Get the inside scoop
on Alberta's self-publishing cookbook business and what happens
when liquor stores cast off the yoke of government monopoly.
What are the best cooking schools in the province, and where do
you go if you need a krumkakker? Meet the people who cater to
the caterers, who brew some of the finest beer in Canada, and
who know which cut of ostrich to serve to a dyed-in-the-wool
beef eater. From organic farmers' markets to roadside diners to
high-end chocolate, it's all here. And yes, there are recipes, too.

The Food Lover's Trail Guide to Alberta is the essential travelling
companion for tourists and locals alike. Packed with timely information, and written by two of Alberta's most trusted food writers,
The Food Lover's Trail Guide to Alberta is a must for every glove
compartment, briefcase, and bookshelf.

THE FOOD LOVER'S TRAIL GUIDE TO ALBERTA
BY MARY BAILEY & JUDY SCHULTZ
AVAILABLE IN BOOKSTORES • WWW.BLUECOUCHBOOKS.COM
6 X 9 PAPERBACK • 256 PAGES • $22.95 CDN • $16.95 US